VERSE AND WORSE • GRAHAM, HARRY

PAGE	
Author's Preface ix	1
Foreword xi	2

PART I
THE BABY'S BAEDEKER

i. Abroad 3	2
ii. United States of America 6	3
iii. Great Britain 9	3
iv. Scotland 11	3
v. Ireland 13	3
vi. Wales 15	3
vii. China 16	3
viii. France 19	4
ix. Germany 21	4
x. Holland 23	4
xi. Iceland 26	4
xii. Italy 27	5
xiii. Japan 30	5
xiv. Portugal 32	5
xv. Russia 33	5
xvi. Spain 36	5
xvii. Switzerland 39	6
xviii. Turkey 41	6
xix. Dreamland 44	6
xx. Stageland 47	6
xxi. Loverland 48	7
xxii. Homeland 53	7

PART II
CHILDISH COMPLAINTS AND OTHER RUTHLESS RHYMES

Childish Complaints —

Prelude 57	7
Appendicitis 61	8
Whooping-Cough 61	8
Measles 62	8
Adenoids 62	8
Croup 62	8

Ruthless Rhymes —

i. Mother-Wit 63	8
ii. Uncle Joe 64	8
iii. Aunt Eliza 65	8
iv. Absent-mindedness 66	8
v. John 68	8
vi. Baby 71	8
vii. The Cat 72	9

PART III
PERVERTED PROVERBS

i. 'Virtue is its own Reward' 77	9
ii. 'Enough is as Good as a Feast' 86	10
iii. 'Don't Buy a Pig in a Poke' 89	10
iv. 'Learn to Take Things Easily' 91	10
v. 'A Rolling Stone Gathers no Moss' 92	10
vi. 'It is Never Too Late to Mend' 96	11
vii. 'A Bad Workman Complains of his Tools' 99	11
viii. 'Don't Look a Gift-horse in the Mouth' 100	11
ix. Potpourri 103	11

PART IV
OTHER VERSES

Bill 111	12
The Legend of the Author 114	12
The Motriot 128	15
The Ballad of the Artist 130	15
The Ballad of Ping-pong 135	16
The Pessimist 138	16
The Place where the Old Cleek Broke 140	16
The Homes of London 143	16
The Happiest Land 146	17
A London Involuntary 151	17
Bluebeard 154	18
The Woman with the Dead Soles 166	19
Rosemary (A Ballad of the Boudoir) 170	19
Portknockie's Porter 172	20
The Ballad of the Little Jinglander 176	20
Aftword 182	21
Envoi 185	21

Publisher's Note

Purchase of this book entitles you to a free trial membership in the publisher's book club at www.rarebooksclub.com. (Time limited offer.) Simply enter the barcode number from the back cover onto the membership form on our home page. The book club entitles you to select from millions of books at no additional charge. You can also download a digital copy of this and related books to read on the go. Simply enter the title or subject onto the search form to find them.

Note: This is an historic book. Pages numbers, where present in the text, refer to the first edition of the book and may also be in indexes.

If you have any questions, could you please be so kind as to consult our Frequently Asked Questions page at www.rarebooksclub.com/faqs.cfm? You are also welcome to contact us there. Publisher: General Books LLC™, Memphis, TN, USA, 2012. ISBN: 9780217979269.
Proofreading: pgdp.net

⁂ ⁂ ⁂ ⁂ ⁂ ⁂ ⁂ ⁂

VERSE AND WORSE

VERSE AND WORSE

VERSE AND WORSE

BY
HARRY GRAHAM
('COL. D. STREAMER')
AUTHOR OF 'BALLADS OF THE BOER WAR,' 'RUTHLESS RHYMES FOR HEARTLESS HOMES,' 'MIS-REPRESENTATIVE MEN,'
'FISCAL BALLADS,' ETC., ETC.
LONDON
EDWARD ARNOLD
41 & 43 MADDOX STREET, BOND STREET, W.
1905
[*All rights reserved*]

NOTE

The Baby's Baedeker and Perverted Proverbs have been published in America by Mr. R. H. Russell and Messrs. Harper Bros. of New York.

'The Ballad of Ping-pong,' 'Bill,' and 'The Place where the Old Cleek Broke,' have appeared in *The Century Magazine*, *The Outlook*, and *Golf* respectively.

'Uncle Joe,' 'Aunt Eliza,' 'John,' 'The Cat,' and 'Bluebeard,' were included in Mr. Russell's American edition of *Ruthless Rhymes for Heartless Homes*.
[Pg v]

[Pg ix]

AUTHOR'S PREFACE

With guilty, conscience-stricken tears,
I offer up these rhymes of mine
To children of maturer years
(From Seventeen to Ninety-nine).
A special solace may they be
In days of second infancy.
The frenzied mother who observes
This volume in her offspring's hand,
And trembles for the darling's nerves,
Must please to clearly understand,
If baby suffers by and by
The Publisher's at fault, not *I*! [Pg x]
But should the little brat survive,
And fatten on this style of Rhyme,
To raise a Heartless Home and thrive
Through a successful life of crime,
The Publisher would have you see
That *I* am to be thanked, not *he*!
Fond parent, you whose children are
Of tender age (from two to eight),
Pray keep this little volume far
From reach of such, and relegate
My verses to an upper shelf;
Where you may study them yourself.
[Pg xi]

FOREWORD

The Press may pass my Verses by
With sentiments of indignation,
And say, like Greeks of old, that I
Corrupt the Youthful Generation;
I am unmoved by taunts like these—
(And so, I think, was Socrates).
Howe'er the Critics may revile,
I pick no journalistic quarrels,
Quite realising that my Style
Makes up for any lack of Morals;
For which I feel no shred of shame—
(And Byron would have felt the same).
[Pg xii]
I don't intend a Child to read
These lines, which are not for the Young;
For, if I did, I should indeed
Feel fully worthy to be hung.
(Is 'hanged' the perfect tense of 'hang'?
Correct me, Mr. Andrew Lang!)
O Young of Heart, tho' in your prime,
By you these verses may be seen!
Accept the Moral with the Rhyme,
And try to gather what I mean.
But, if you can't, it won't hurt me!
(And Browning would, I know, agree.)
Be reassured, I have not got
The style of Stephen Phillips' heroes,
Nor Henry Jones's pow'r of Plot,
Nor wit like Arthur Wing Pinero's!
(If so, I should not waste my time
In writing you this sort of rhyme.)
[Pg xiii]
I strive to paint things as they Are,
Of Realism the true Apostle;
All flow'ry metaphors I bar,
Nor call the homely thrush a 'throstle.'
Such synonyms would make me smile.
(And so they would have made Carlyle.)
My Style may be, at times, I own,
A trifle cryptic or abstruse;
In this I do not stand alone,
And need but mention, in excuse,
A thousand world-familiar names,
From Meredith to Henry James.
From these my fruitless fancy roams
To Aesop's or La Fontaine's Fable,
From Doyle's or Hemans' 'Stately Ho(l)mes,'
To t'other of The Breakfast Table;
Like Galahad, I wish (in vain)
'My wit were as the wit of Twain!
[Pg xiv]
Had I but Whitman's rugged skill,
(And managed to escape the Censor),
The Accuracy of a Mill,
The Reason of a Herbert Spencer,
The literary talents even
Of Sidney Lee or Leslie Stephen,
The pow'r of Patmore's placid pen,
Or Watson's gift of execration,
The sugar of Le Gallienne,
Or Algernon's alliteration,
One post there is I'd not be lost in,
—Tho' I might find it most ex-Austin'!
Some day, if I but study hard,
The public, vanquished by my pen, 'll
Acclaim me as a Minor Bard,
Like Norman Gale or Mrs. Meynell;
And listen to my lyre a-rippling
Imperial banjo-spasms like Kipling.
[Pg xv]
Were I, like him, a syndicate,
Which publishers would put their trust in;
A Walter Pater up-to-date,
Or flippant scholar like Augustine;
With pen as light as lark or squirrel,
I'd love to kipple, pate and birrell.
So don't ignore me. If you should,
'Twill touch me to the very heart oh!
To be as much misunderstood
As once was Andrea del Sarto;
Unrecognised, to toil away,
Like Millet,—(not, of course, Mill*ais*).
And, pray, for Morals do not look
In this unique agglomeration,
—This unpretentious little book
Of Infelicitous Quotation.
I deem you foolish if you do,
(And Mr. Arnold thinks so, too).
[Pg 1]

PART I

THE BABY'S BAEDEKER

An International Guide-Book for the young of all ages;
peculiarly adapted to the wants of first and second Childhood.
[Pg 3]

I

ABROAD

Abroad is where we tourists spend,
In divers unalluring ways,
The brief occasional week-end,
Or annual Easter holidays;
And earn the (not ill-founded) charge
Of being lunatics at large.
Abroad, we lose our self-respect;
Wear whiskers; let our teeth protrude;
Consider any garb correct,
And no display of temper rude;
Descending, when we cross the foam,
To depths we dare not plumb at home.
[Pg 4]
(Small wonder that the natives gaze,
With hostile eyes, at foreign freaks,
Who patronise their Passion-plays,
In lemon-coloured chessboard breeks;
An op'ra-glass about each neck,
And on each head a cap of check.)
Abroad, where needy younger sons,
When void the parent's treasure-chest,
Take refuge from insistent duns,
At urgent relatives' request;
To live upon their slender wits,
Or sums some maiden-aunt remits.
Abroad, whence (with a wisdom rare)
Regardless of nostalgic pains,
The weary New York millionaire
Retires with his oil-gotten gains,
And learns how deep a pleasure 'tis
To found our Public Libraries.
[Pg 5]

For ours is the primeval clan,
From which all lesser lights descend;
Is Crockett not our countryman?
And call we not Corelli friend?
Our brotherhood has bred the brain
Whose offspring bear the brand of Caine.
Tho' nowadays we seldom hear
Miss Proctor, who mislaid a chord,
Or Tennyson, the poet peer,
Who came into the garden, Mord;
Tho' Burns be dead, and Keats unread,
We have a prophet still in Stead.
And so we stare, with nose in air;
And speak in condescending tone,
Of foreigners whose climes compare
So favourably with our own;
And aliens we cannot applaud
Who call themselves At Home Abroad!
[Pg 6]

II

UNITED STATES OF AMERICA

This is the Country of the Free,
The Cocktail and the Ten Cent Chew;
Where you're as good a man as me,
And I'm a better man than you!
(O Liberty, how free we make!
Freedom, what liberties we take!)
'Tis here the startled tourist meets,
'Mid clanging of a thousand bells,
The railways running through the streets,
Skyscraping flats and vast hotels,
Where rest, on the resplendent floors,
The necessary cuspidors.
[Pg 7]
And here you may encounter too
The pauper immigrants in shoals,
The Swede, the German, and the Jew,
The Irishman, who rules the polls
And is employed to keep the peace,
A venal and corrupt police.
They are so busy here, you know,
They have no time at all for play;
Each morning to their work they go
And stay there all the livelong day;
Their dreams of happiness depend
On making more than they can spend.
The ladies of this land are all
Developed to a pitch sublime,
Some inches over six foot tall,
With perfect figures all the time.
(For further notice of their looks
See Mr. Dana Gibson's books.)
[Pg 8]
And, if they happen to possess
Sufficient balance at the bank,
They have the chance of saying 'Yes!'
To needy foreigners of rank;
The future dukes of all the earth
Are half American by birth.
MORAL
A 'dot' combining cash with charms
Is worth a thousand coats-of-arms.
[Pg 9]

III

GREAT BRITAIN

The British are a chilly race.
The Englishman is thin and tall;
He screws an eyeglass in his face,
And talks with a reluctant drawl.
'Good Gwacious! This is doosid slow!
By Jove! Haw demmy! Don't-cher-know!'
The English*woman* ev'rywhere
A meed of admiration wins;
She has a crown of silken hair,
And quite the loveliest of skins.
(Go forth and seek an English maid,
Your trouble will be well repaid.)
[Pg 10]
Where Britain's banner is unfurled
There's room for nothing else beside,
She owns one-quarter of the world,
And still she is not satisfied.
The Briton thinks himself, by birth,
To be the lord of all the earth.
Some call his manners wanting, or
His sense of humour poor, and yet
Whatever he is striving for
He as a rule contrives to get;
His methods may be much to blame,
But he arrives there just the same.
MORAL
If you can get your wish, you bet it
Doesn't much matter *how* you get it!
[Pg 11]

IV

SCOTLAND

In Scotland all the people wear
Red hair and freckles, and one sees
The men in women's dresses there,
With stout, décolleté, low-necked knees.
('Eblins ye dinna ken, I doot,
We're unco guid, so hoot, mon, hoot!')
They love 'ta whuskey' and 'ta Kirk';
I don't know which they like the most.
They aren't the least afraid of work;
No sense of humour can they boast;
And you require an axe to coax
The canny Scot to see your jokes.
[Pg 12]
They play an instrument they call
The bagpipes; and the sound of these
Is reminiscent of the squall
Of infant pigs attacked by bees;
Music that might drive cats away
Or make reluctant chickens lay.
MORAL
Wear kilts, and, tho' men look askance,
Go out and give your knees a chance.
[Pg 13]

V

IRELAND

The Irishman is never quite
Contented with his little lot;
He's ever thirsting for a fight,
A grievance he has always got;
And all his energy is bent
On trying not to pay his rent.
He lives upon a frugal fare
(The few potatoes that he digs),
And hospitably loves to share
His bedroom with his wife and pigs;
But cannot settle even here,
And gets evicted once a year.
[Pg 14]
In order to amuse himself,
At any time when things are slack,
He takes his gun down from the shelf
And shoots a landlord in the back;
If he is lucky in the chase,
He may contrive to bag a brace.
MORAL
Procure a grievance and a gun
And you can have no end of fun.
[Pg 15]

VI

WALES

The natives of the land of Wales
Are not a very truthful lot,
And the imagination fails
To paint the language they have got;
Bettws-y-coed-llan-dud-nod-
Dolgelly-rhiwlas-cwn-wm-dod!
MORAL
If you *must* talk, then do it, pray,
In an intelligible way.
[Pg 16]

VII

CHINA

The Chinaman from early youth
Is by his wise preceptors taught
To have no dealings with the Truth,
In fact, romancing is his 'forte.'
In juggling words he takes the prize,
By the sheer beauty of his lies.
For laundrywork he has a knack;
He takes in shirts and makes them blue;
When he omits to send them back
He takes his customers in too.
He must be ranked in the 'élite'
Of those whose hobby is deceit.
[Pg 17]
For ladies 'tis the fashion here
To pinch their feet and make them small,
Which, to the civilised idea,
Is not a proper thing at all.
Our modern Western woman's taste
In pinching leans towards the waist.
The Chinese Empire is the field
Where foreign missionaries go;
A poor result their labours yield,
And they have little fruit to show;
For, if you would convert Wun Lung,
You have to catch him very young.
The Chinaman has got a creed
And a religion of his own,
And would be much obliged indeed
If you could leave his soul alone;
And he prefers, which may seem odd,
His own to other people's god.
[Pg 18]
Yet still the missionary tries
To point him out his wickedness,
Until the badgered natives rise,—
And there's one missionary less!
Then foreign Pow'rs step in, you see,
And ask for an indemnity.
MORAL
Adhere to facts, avoid romance,
And you a clergyman may be;
To lie is wrong, except perchance
In matters of Diplomacy.
And, when you start out to convert,
Make certain that you don't get hurt!
[Pg 19]

VIII

FRANCE

The natives here remark 'Mon Dieu!'
'Que voulez-vous?' 'Comment ça va?'
'Sapristi! Par exemple! Un peu!'
'Tiens donc! Mais qu'est-ce que c'est que ça?'
They shave one portion of their dogs,
And live exclusively on frogs.
They get excited very quick,
And crowds will gather before long
If you should stand and wave your stick
And shout, 'À bas le Presidong!'
Still more amusing would it be
To say, 'Conspuez la Patrie!'
[Pg 20]
The French are so polite, you know,
They take their hats off very well,
And, should they tread upon your toe,
Remark, 'Pardon, Mademoiselle!'
And you would gladly bear the pain
To see them make that bow again.
Their ladies too have got a way
Which even curates can't resist;
'Twould make an Alderman feel gay
Or soothe a yellow journalist;
And then the things they say are so
Extremely—well, in fact,—you know!
MORAL
The closest scrutiny can find
No morals here of any kind.
[Pg 21]

IX

GERMANY

The German is a stolid soul,
And finds best suited to his taste
A pipe with an enormous bowl,
A fraulein with an ample waist;
He loves his beer, his Kaiser, and
(Donner und blitz!) his Fatherland!
He's perfectly contented if
He listens in the Op'ra-house
To Wagner's well-concealed 'motif,'
Or waltzes of the nimble Strauss;
And all discordant bands he sends
Abroad, to soothe his foreign friends.
[Pg 22]
When he is glad at anything
He cheers like a dyspeptic goat,
'Hoch! hoch!' You'd think him suffering
From some affection of the throat.
A disagreeable noise, 'tis true,
But pleases him and don't hurt you!
MORAL
A glass of lager underneath the bough,
A long 'churchwarden' and an ample 'frau'
Beside me sitting in a Biergarten,
Ach! Biergarten were paradise enow!
[Pg 23]

X

HOLLAND

This country is extremely flat,
Just like your father's head, and were
It not for dykes and things like that
There would not be much country there,
For, if these banks should broken be,
What now is land would soon be sea.
So, any child who glory seeks,
And in a dyke observes a hole,
Must hold his finger there for weeks,
And keep the water from its goal,
Until the local plumbers come,
Or other persons who can plumb.
[Pg 24]
The Hollanders have somehow got
The name of Dutch (why, goodness knows!),
But Mrs. Hollander is not
A 'duchess' as you might suppose;
Mynheer Von Vanderpump is much
More used to style her his 'Old Dutch.'
Their cities' names are somewhat odd,
But much in vogue with golfing men
Who miss a 'put' or slice a sod,
(Whose thoughts I would not dare to pen),
'Oh, Rotterdam!' they can exclaim,
And blamelessly resume the game.
The Dutchman's dress is very neat;
He minds his little flock of goats
In cotton blouse, and on his feet
He dons a pair of wooden boats.
(He evidently does not trust
Those dykes I mentioned not to bust).
[Pg 25]
He has the reputation too
Of being what is known as 'slim,'
Which merely means he does to you
What you had hoped to do to him;
He has a business head, that's all,
And takes some beating, does Oom Paul.
MORAL
Avoid a country where the sea
May any day drop in to tea,
Rememb'ring that, at golf, one touch
Of bunker makes the whole world Dutch!
[Pg 26]

XI

ICELAND

The climate is intensely cold;
Wild curates would not drag me there;
Not tho' they brought great bags of gold,
And piled them underneath my chair.
If twenty bishops bade me go,
I should decidedly say, 'No!'
MORAL
If ev'ry man has got his price,
As generally is agreed,
You will, by taking my advice,
Let yours be very large indeed.
Corruption is not nice at all,
Unless the bribe be far from small.
[Pg 27]

XII

ITALY

In Italy the sky is blue;
The native loafs and lolls about,
He's nothing in the world to do,
And does it fairly well, no doubt;
(Ital-i-ans are disinclined
To honest work of any kind).
A light Chianti wine he drinks,
And fancies it extremely good;
(It tastes like Stephens' Blue-black Inks);—
While macaroni is his food.
(I think it must be rather hard
To eat one's breakfast by the yard).
[Pg 28]
And, when he leaves his country for
Some northern climate, 'tis his dream
To be an organ grinder, or
Retail bacilli in ice-cream.
(The French or German student terms
These creatures '*Paris*ites' or '*Germs*.')
Sometimes an anarchist is he,
And wants to slay a king or queen;
So with some dynamite, may be,
Concocts a murderous machine;
'Here goes!' he shouts, 'For Freedom's sake!'
Then blows himself up by mistake.
Naples and Florence both repay
A visit, and, if fortune takes
Your toddling little feet that way,
Do stop a moment at The Lakes.
While, should you go to Rome, I hope
You'll leave your card upon the Pope.
[Pg 29]
MORAL
Don't work too hard, but use a wise discretion;
Adopt the least laborious profession.
Don't be an anarchist, but, if you must,
Don't let your bombshell prematurely bust.
[Pg 30]

XIII

JAPAN

Inhabitants of far Japan
Are happy as the day is long
To sit behind a paper fan
And sing a kind of tuneless song,
Desisting, ev'ry little while,
To have a public bath, or smile.
The members of the fairer sex
Are clad in a becoming dress,
One garment reaching from their necks
Down to the ankles more or less;
Behind each dainty ear they wear
A cherry-blossom in their hair.
[Pg 31]
If 'Imitation's flattery'
(We learn it at our mother's lap),
A flatterer by birth must be
Our clever little friend the Jap,
Who does whatever we can do,
And does it rather better too.
MORAL
Be happy all the time, and plan
To wash as often as you can.
[Pg 32]

XIV

PORTUGAL

You are requested, if you please,
To note that here a people lives
Referred to as the Portuguese;
A fact which naturally gives
The funny man a good excuse
To call his friend a Portugoose.
MORAL
Avoid the obvious, if you can,
And *never* be a funny man.
[Pg 33]

XV

RUSSIA

The Russian Empire, as you see,
Is governed by an Autocrat,
A sort of human target he
For anarchists to practise at;
And much relieved most people are
Not to be lodging with the Czar.
The Russian lets his whiskers grow,
Smokes cigarettes at meal-times, and
Imbibes more 'vodki' than 'il faut';
A habit which (I understand)
Enables him with ease to tell
His name, which nobody could spell.
[Pg 34]
The climate here is cold, with snow,
And you go driving in a sleigh,
With bells and all the rest, you know,
Just like a Henry Irving play;
While, all around you, glare the eyes
Of secret officers and spies!
The Russian prisons have no drains,
No windows or such things as that;
You have no playthings there but chains,
And no companion but a rat;
When once behind the dungeon door,
Your friends don't see you any more.
I further could enlarge, 'tis true,
But fear my trembling pen confines;
I have no wish to travel to
Siberia and work the mines.
(In Russia you must write with care,
Or the police will take you there.)
[Pg 35]
MORAL
If you hold morbid views about
A monarch's premature decease,
You only need a—Hi! Look out!
Here comes an agent of police!
. . . . .
(In future my address will be
'Siberia, Cell 63.')
[Pg 36]

XVI

SPAIN

'Tis here the Spanish onion grows,
And they eat garlic all the day,
So, if you have a tender nose,
'Tis best to go the other way,
Or else you may discern, at length,
The fact that 'Onion is strength.'
The chestnuts flourish in this land,
Quite good to eat, as you will find,
For they are not, you understand,
The ancient after-dinner kind
That Yankees are accustomed to
From Mr. Chauncey M. Depew.
[Pg 37]
The Spanish lady, by the bye,

Is an alluring person who
Has got a bright and flashing eye,
And knows just how to use it too;
It's quite a treat to see her meet
The proud hidalgo on the street.
He wears a sort of soft felt hat,
A dagger, and a cloak, you know,
Just like the wicked villains that
We met in plays of long ago,
Who sneaked about with aspect glum,
Remarking, 'Ha! A time will come!'
His blood, of blue cerulean hue,
Runs in his veins like liquid fire,
And he can be most rude if you
Should rob him of his heart's desire;
'Caramba!' he exclaims, and whack!
His dagger perforates your back!
[Pg 38]
If you should care to patronise
A bull-fight, as you will no doubt,
You'll see a horse with blinded eyes
Be very badly mauled about;
By such a scene a weak inside
Is sometimes rather sorely tried.
And, if the bull is full of fun,
The horse is generally gored,
So then they fetch another one,
Or else the first one is encored;
The humour of the sport, of course,
Is not so patent to the horse.
MORAL
Be kind to ev'ry bull you meet,
Remember how the creature feels;
Don't wink at ladies in the street;
And don't make speeches after meals;
And lastly, I need not explain,
If you're a horse, don't go to Spain.
[Pg 39]

XVII

SWITZERLAND

This atmosphere is pure ozone!
To climb the hills you promptly start;
Unless you happen to be prone
To palpitations of the heart;
In which case swarming up the Alps
Brings on a bad attack of palps.
The nicest method is to stay
Quite comfortably down below,
And, from the steps of your chalet,
Watch other people upwards go.
Then you can buy an alpenstock,
And scratch your name upon a rock.
[Pg 40]
MORAL

Don't do fatiguing things which you
Can pay another man to do.
Let friends assume (they may be wrong),
That you each year ascend Mong Blong.
Some things you can *pretend* you've done,
And climbing up the Alps is one.
[Pg 41]

XVIII

TURKEY

The Sultan of the Purple East
Is quite a cynic, in his way,
And really doesn't mind the least
His nickname of 'Abdul the ——'
(Nay!
I might perhaps come in for blame
If I divulged this monarch's name.)
The Turk is such a kindly man,
But his ideas of sport are crude;
He to the poor Armenian
Is not intentionally rude,
But still it is his heartless habit
To treat him as *we* treat the rabbit.
[Pg 42]
If he wants bracing up a bit,
His pleasing little custom is
To take a hatchet and commit
A series of atrocities.
I should not fancy, after dark,
To meet him, say, in Regent's Park.
A deeply married man is he,
'Early and often' is his rule;
He practises polygamy
Directly after leaving school,
And so arranges that his wives
Live happy but secluded lives.
If they attend a public place,
They have to do so in disguise,
And so conceal one-half their face
That nothing but a pair of eyes
Suggests the hidden charm that lurks
Beneath the veils of lady Turks.
[Pg 43]
Then too in Turkey all the men
Smoke water-pipes and cross their legs;
They watch their harem as a hen
That guards her first attempt at eggs.
(If you don't know what harems are,
Just run and ask your dear papa.)
MORAL
Wives of great men oft remind us
We should make our wives sublime,
But the years advancing find us
Vainly working over-time.
We could minimise our work
By the methods of the Turk.
[Pg 44]

XIX

DREAMLAND

Here you will see strange happenings
With absolutely placid eyes;
If all your uncles sprouted wings
You would not feel the least surprise;
The oddest things that you can do
Don't seem a bit absurd to you.
You go (in Dreamland) to a ball,
And suddenly are shocked to find
That you have nothing on at all,—
But somehow no one seems to mind;
And, naturally, *you* don't care,
If they can bear what you can bare!
[Pg 45]
Then, in a moment, you're pursued
By engines on a railway track!
Your legs are tied, your feet are glued,
The train comes snorting down your back!
One last attempt at flight you make
And so (in bed) perspiring wake.
You feel so free from weight of cares
That, if the staircase you should climb,
You gaily mount, not single stairs,
But whole battalions at a time;
(My metaphor is mixed, may be,
I quote from Shakespeare, as you see).
If you should eat too much, you pay
(In dreams) the penalty for this;
A nightmare carries you away
And drops you down a precipice!
[Pg 46] Down! down! until, with sudden smack,
You strike the mattress with your back.
MORAL
At meals decline to be a beast;
'Too much is better than a feast.'
[Pg 47]

XX

STAGELAND

The customs of this land have all
Been published in a bulky tome.
The author is a man they call
Jer*ome* K. Jer*ome* K. Jer*ome*.
So, lest on his preserves I poach,
This subject I refuse to broach.
MORAL
The moral here is plain to see.

If true the hackneyed witticism
Which stamps Originality
As 'undetected plagiarism,'
What a vocation I have miss'd
As undetected plagiarist!
[Pg 48]

XXI

LOVERLAND

This is the land where minor bards
And other lunatics repair,
To live in houses made of cards,
Or build their castles in the air;
To feed on hope, and idly dream
That things are really what they seem.
The natives are a motley lot,
Of ev'ry age and creed and race,
But each inhabitant has got
The same expression on his face;
They look, when this their features fills,
Like angels with internal chills.
[Pg 49]
The lover sits, the livelong day,
Quite inarticulate of speech;
He simply brims with things to say;
Alas! the words he cannot reach,
And, silent, lets occasion pass,
Feeling a fulminating ass.
It is the lady lover's wont
To blush, and look demure or coy,
To say, 'You mustn't!' and, 'Oh! don't!'
Or, 'Please leave off, you naughty boy!'
(But this, of course, is just her way,
She wouldn't wish you to obey.)
The lover, in a trembling voice,
Demands the hand of his lovee,
And begs the lady of his choice
To share some cottage-by-the-sea;
With *her* a prison would be nice,
A coal-cellar a Paradise!
[Pg 50]
'Love in a cottage' sounds so well;
But oh, my too impatient bride,
No drainage and a constant smell
Of something being over-fried
Is not the sort of atmosphere
That makes for wedded bliss, my dear.
And when the bills are rather high,
And when the money's rather low,
See poor Virginia sit and sigh,
And ask why Paul *must* grumble so!
He slams the door and strides about,
And, through the window, Love creeps out.

'Tis said that Cupid blinds our sight
With fire of passion from above,
Nor ever bids us see aright
The many faults in those we love;
Ah no! I deem it otherwise,
For lovers have the clearest eyes.
[Pg 51]
They see the faults, the failures, and
The great temptations, and they know,
Although they cannot understand,
That they would have the loved one so.
Believe me, Love is never blind,
His smiling eyes are wise and kind.
Tho' lovers quarrel, yet, I ween,
'Tis but to make it up again;
The sunshine seems the more serene
That follows after April rain;
And love should lead, if love be true,
To perfect understanding too.
If in our hearts this love beats strong,
We shall not ever seek to earn
Forgiveness for some fancied wrong,
Nor need to pardon in return;
But learn this lesson as we live,
'To understand is to forgive.'
[Pg 52]
And all you little girls and boys
Will find this out yourselves, some day,
When you have done with childish toys
And put your infant books away.
Ah! then I pray that hand-in-hand
You tread the paths of Loverland.
MORAL
Don't fall in love, but, when you do,
Take care that he (or she) does too;
And, lastly, to misquote the bard,
If you *must* love, don't love too hard.
[Pg 53]

XXII

HOMELAND

The tour is over! We must part!
Our mutual journey at an end.
O bid farewell, with aching heart,
To guide, philosopher, and friend;
And note, as you remark 'Good-bye!'
The kindly tear that dims his eye.
The tour is ended! Sad but true!
No more together may we roam!
We turn our lonely footsteps to
The spot that's known as Home, Sweet Home.
Nor time nor temper can afford
A more protracted trip abroad.
[Pg 54]

O Home! where we must always be
So hopelessly misunderstood;
Where waits a tactless family,
To tell us things 'for our own good';
Where relatives, with searchlight eyes,
Can penetrate our choicest lies.
Where all our kith and kin combine
To prove that we are worse than rude,
If we should criticise the wine
Or make complaints about the food.
Thank goodness, then, to quote the pome,
Thank goodness there's 'no place like Home!'
[Pg 55]

PART II

CHILDISH COMPLAINTS
AND
OTHER RUTHLESS RHYMES
[Pg 57]

CHILDISH COMPLAINTS

PRELUDE

(*By Way of Advertisement*)
I have no knowledge of disease,
No notion what ill-health may be,
Since Housemaid's Throat and Smoker's Knees
Mean something different to me
To what they do to other folk.
(This is, I vow, no vulgar joke.)
Of course, when young, I had complaints,
And little childish accidents;
For twice I ate a box of paints,
And once I swallowed eighteen pence.
(*N.B.*, I missed the paints a lot,
But got the coins back on the spot.)
[Pg 58]
But no practitioner has seen
My tongue since then, down to the present,
And I, alas! have never been
An interesting convalescent.
Ah! why am I alone denied
The Humour of a weak inside?
Why is it? I will tell you why;
A certain mixture is to blame.
One day for fun I chanced to try
A bottle of—what *is* the name?
That thing they advertise a lot,—
(Oh, what a memory I've got!)
It's stuff you must, of course, have seen,

Retailed in bottles, tins, or pots,
In cakes or little pills, I mean—
(Oh goodness me! I've bought such lots,
That I am really much to blame
For not remembering the name!)
[Pg 59]
Still, let me recommend a keg
(With maker's name, be sure, above it),
'Tis sweeter than a new-mown egg,
And village idiots simply love it;
Old persons sit and scream for it,—
I do so hope you'll try a bit!
So efficacious is this stuff,
Its virtue and its strength are such,
One single bottle is enough,—
In fact, at times, 'tis far too much.
(The patient dies in frightful pain,
Or else survives, and tries again.)
An aunt of mine felt anyhow,
All kind-of-odd, and gone-to-bits,
Had freckles badly too; but now
She doesn't have a thing but fits.
She's just as strong as any horse,—
Tho' still an invalid, of course.
[Pg 60]
I had an uncle, too, that way,
His health was in a dreadful plight;
Would often spend a sleepless day,
And lie unconscious half the night.
He took two bottles, large and small,
And now—he has no health at all!
The Moral plainly bids you buy
This stuff, whose name I have forgotten;
You won't regret it, if you try—
(My memory is simply rotten!)
My funds will profit, in addition,
Since I enjoy a small commission!
[Pg 61]

CHILDISH COMPLAINTS

No. 1 (Appendicitis)

I've got Appendicitis
In my Appendicit,
But I don't mind,
Because I find
I'm quite 'cut out' for it.

No. 2 (Whooping-cough)

If only I had Whooping-cough!
I'd join a Circus troupe!
And folks would clamour at the door,
And pay a shilling—even more,
To see me 'Whoop The Whoop.'

[Pg 62]

No. 3. (Measles)

Of illnesses like chickenpox
And measles I've had lots;
I do not like them much, you know,
They are not really nice, altho'
They're rather nice in spots.

No. 4. (Adenoids)

A Cockney maid produced such snores,
Folks left the City to avoid them;
And all becos,
She said, it was
Her adenoids that 'ad annoyed them!

No. 5. (Croup)

I had the Croup, in years gone by,
And that is why to-day,
Altho' no longer youthful, I
Am still a Croupier.
[Pg 63]

RUTHLESS RHYMES

I
MOTHER-WIT

When wilful little Willie Black
Threw all the tea-things at his mother,
She murmured, as she hurled them back,
'One good Tea-urn deserves another!'
[Pg 64]

II
UNCLE JOE

Poor Uncle Joe has gone, you know,
To rest beyond the stars.
I miss him, oh! I miss him so,—
He had *such* good cigars.
[Pg 65]

III
AUNT ELIZA

In the drinking-well
(Which the plumber built her)
Aunt Eliza fell,——
We must buy a filter.
[Pg 66]

IV
ABSENT-MINDEDNESS

Absent-minded Edward Brown
Drove his lady into town;
Suddenly the horse fell down!
Mrs. Ned
(Newly wed)
Threw a fit and lay for dead.
Edward, lacking in resource,
Chafed the fetlocks of his horse,
Sitting with unpleasant force
(Just like lead)
On the head
Of the prostrate Mrs. Ned.
[Pg 67]
She demanded a divorce,
Jealous of the favoured horse.
Edward had it shot, of course.
. . . . .
Years have sped;
She and Ned
Drive a motor now instead.
[Pg 68]

V
JOHN

John, across the broad Atlantic,
Tried to navigate a barque,
But he met an unromantic
And extremely hungry shark.
John (I blame his childhood's teachers)
Thought to treat this as a lark,
Ignorant of how these creatures
Do delight to bite a barque.
Said, 'This animal's a bore!' and,
With a scornful sort of grin,
Handled an adjacent oar and
Chucked it underneath the chin.
[Pg 69]
At this unexpected juncture,
Which he had not reckoned on,
Mr. Shark he made a puncture
In the barque—and then in John.
. . . . .
Sad am I, and sore at thinking
John had on some clothes of mine;
I can almost see them shrinking,
Washed repeatedly in brine.
I shall never cease regretting
That I lent my hat to him,
For I fear a thorough wetting
Cannot well improve the brim.
Oh! to know a shark is browsing,
Boldly, blandly, on my boots!
Coldly, cruelly carousing
On the choicest of my suits!
[Pg 70]
Creatures I regard with loathing,
Who can calmly take their fill
Of one's Jaeger underclothing:—
Down, my aching heart, be still!
[Pg 71]

VI
BABY

Baby roused its father's ire,
By a cold and formal lisp;
So he placed it on the fire,
And reduced it to a crisp.
Mother said, 'Oh, stop a bit!
This is *overdoing* it!'
[Pg 72]

VII
THE CAT

(*Advice to the Young*)

My children, you should imitate
The harmless, necessary cat,
Who eats whatever's on his plate,
And doesn't even leave the fat;
Who never stays in bed too late,
Or does immoral things like that;
Instead of saying, 'Shan't!' or 'Bosh!'
He'll sit and wash, and wash, and wash!
[Pg 73]

When shadows fall and lights grow dim,
He sits beneath the kitchen stair;
Regardless as to life and limb,
A shady lair he chooses there;
And if you tumble over him,
He simply loves to hear you swear.
And, while bad language *you* prefer,
He'll sit and purr, and purr, and purr!
[Pg 75]

PART III
PERVERTED PROVERBS
[Pg 77]

I
'VIRTUE IS ITS OWN REWARD'

Virtue its own reward? Alas!
And what a poor one, as a rule!
Be Virtuous, and Life will pass
Like one long term of Sunday-school.
(No prospect, truly, could one find
More unalluring to the mind.)
The Model Child has got to keep
His fingers and his garments white;
In church he may not go to sleep,
Nor ask to stop up late at night.
In fact he must not ever do
A single thing he wishes to.
[Pg 78]

He may not paddle in his boots,
Like naughty children, at the sea;
The sweetness of Forbidden Fruits
Is not, alas! for such as he.
He watches, with pathetic eyes,
His weaker brethren make mud-pies.
He must not answer back, oh no!
However rude grown-ups may be;
But keep politely silent, tho'
He brim with scathing repartee;
For nothing is considered worse
Than scoring off Mamma or Nurse.
He must not eat too much at meals,
Nor scatter crumbs upon the floor;
However vacuous he feels,
He may not pass his plate for more;
—Not tho' his ev'ry organ ache
For further slabs of Christmas cake.
[Pg 79]
He is commanded not to waste
The fleeting hours of childhood's days,
By giving way to any taste
For circuses or matinées;
For him the entertainments planned
Are 'Lectures on the Holy Land.'
He never reads a story-book
By Rider H. or Winston C.,
In vain upon his desk you'd look
For tales by Arthur Conan D.,
Nor could you find upon his shelf
The works of Rudyard—or myself!
He always fears that he may do
Some action that is *infra dig.*,
And so he lives his short life through
In the most noxious rôle of Prig.
('Short Life' I say, for it's agreed
The Good die very young indeed.)
[Pg 80]
Ah me! how sad it is to think
He could have lived like me—or you!
With practice, and a taste for drink,
Our joys he might have known, he too!
And shared the pleasure *we* have had
In being gloriously bad!
The Naughty Boy gets much delight
From doing what he should not do;
But, as such conduct isn't Right,
He sometimes suffers for it, too.
Yet, what's a spanking to the fun
Of leaving vital things Undone?
The Wicked flourish like the bay,
At Cards or Love they always win,
Good Fortune dogs their steps all day,
They fatten while the Good grow thin.
The Righteous Man has much to bear;
The Bad becomes a Bullionaire!
[Pg 81]
For, though he be the greatest sham,
Luck favours him, his whole life through;
At 'Bridge' he always makes a Slam
After declaring 'Sans atout';
With ev'ry deal his fate has planned
A hundred Aces in his hand.
Yes, it is always just the same;
He somehow manages to win,
By mere good fortune, any game
That he may be competing in.
At Golf no bunker breaks his club,
For him the green provides no 'rub.'
At Billiards, too, he flukes away
(With quite unnecessary 'side');
No matter what he tries to play,
For him the pockets open wide;
He never finds both balls in baulk,
Or makes miss-cues for want of chalk.
[Pg 82]
He swears; he very likely bets;
He even wears a flaming necktie;
Inhales Egyptian cigarettes,
And has a 'Mens Inconscia Recti';
Yet, spite of all, one must confess
That nought succeeds like his excess.
There's no occasion to be Just,
No need for motives that are fine,
To be Director of a Trust,
Or Manager of a Combine;
Your Corner is a public curse,
Perhaps, but it will fill your purse.
Then stride across the Public's bones,
Crush all opponents under you,
Until you 'rise on stepping-stones
Of their dead selves'; and, when you do,
The widow's and the orphan's tears
Shall comfort your declining years!
[Pg 83]
. . . . .
Myself, how lucky I must be,
That need not fear so gross an end;
Since Fortune has not favoured me
With many million pounds to spend.
(Still, did that fickle Dame relent,
I'd show you how they *should* be spent!)
I am not saint enough to feel
My shoulder ripen to a wing,
Nor have I wits enough to steal
His title from the Copper King;
And there's a vasty gulf between
The man I Am and Might Have Been;
But tho' at dinner I may take
Too much of Heidsick (extra dry),
And underneath the table make
My simple couch just where I lie,
My mode of roosting on the floor

Is just a trick and nothing more.
[Pg 84]
And when, not Wisely but too Well,
My thirst I have contrived to quench,
The stories I am apt to tell
May be, perhaps, a trifle French;—
(For 'tis in anecdote, no doubt,
That what's Bred in the Beaune comes out.)—
It does not render me unfit
To give advice, both wise and right,
Because I do not follow it
Myself as closely as I might;
There's nothing that I wouldn't do
To point the proper road to *you*.
And this I'm sure of, more or less,
And trust that you will all agree—
The Elements of Happiness
Consist in being—just like Me;
No sinner, nor a saint perhaps,
But—well, the very best of chaps.
[Pg 85]
Share the Experience I have had,
Consider all I've known and seen,
And Don't be Good, and Don't be Bad,
But cultivate a Golden Mean.
. . . . .
What makes Existence *really* nice
Is Virtue—with a dash of Vice.
[Pg 86]

II
'ENOUGH IS AS GOOD AS A FEAST'

What is Enough? An idle dream!
One cannot have enough, I swear,
Of Ices or Meringues-and-Cream,
Nougat or Chocolate Éclairs,
Of Oysters or of Caviar,
Of Prawns or Pâté de Foie *Grar*!
Who would not willingly forsake
Kindred and Home, without a fuss,
For Icing from a Birthday Cake,
Or juicy fat Asparagus,
And journey over countless seas
For New Potatoes and Green Peas?
[Pg 87]
They say that a Contented Mind
Is a Continual Feast;—but where
The mental frame, and how to find,
Which can with Turtle Soup compare?
No mind, however full of Ease,
Could be Continual Toasted Cheese.
For dinner have a sole to eat
(Some Perrier Jouet, '92),
An Entrée then (and, with the meat,
A bottle of Lafitte will do),
A quail, a glass of port (just one),
Liqueurs and coffee, and you've done.
Your tastes may be of simpler type;—
A homely pint of 'half-and-half,'
An onion and a dish of tripe,
Or headpiece of the kindly calf.
(Cruel perhaps, but then, you know,
"*Faut tout souffrir pour être veau*!')
[Pg 88]
'Tis a mistake to eat too much
Of any dishes but the best;
And you, of course, should never touch
A thing you *know* you can't digest;
For instance, lobster:—if you *do*,
Well,—I'm amayonnaised at you!
Let this be your heraldic crest:
A bottle (chargé) of Champagne,
A chicken (gorged) with salad (dress'd),
Below, this motto to explain—
'Enough is Very Good, may be;
Too Much is Good Enough for Me!'
[Pg 89]

III
'DON'T BUY A PIG IN A POKE'

Unscrupulous Pigmongers will
Attempt to wheedle and to coax
The ignorant young housewife till
She purchases her pigs in pokes;
Beasts that have got a Lurid Past,
Or else are far Too Good to Last.
So, should you not desire to be
The victim of a cruel hoax,
Then promise me, ah! promise me,
You will not purchase pigs in pokes!
('Twould be an error just as big
To poke your purchase in a pig.)
[Pg 90]
Too well I know the bitter cost,
To turn this subject off with jokes;
How many fortunes have been lost
By men who purchased pigs in pokes.
(Ah! think on such when you would talk
With mouths that are replete with pork!)
And, after dinner, round the fire,
Astride of Grandpa's rugged knee,
Implore your bored but patient sire
To tell you what a Poke may be.
The fact he might disclose to you—
Which is far more than *I* can do.
. . . . .
The Moral of The Pigs and Pokes
Is not to make your choice too quick.
In purchasing a Book of Jokes,
Pray poke around and take your pick.
Who knows how rich a mental meal
The covers of *this* book conceal?
[Pg 91]

IV
'LEARN TO TAKE THINGS EASILY'

To these few words, it seems to me,
A wealth of sound instruction clings;
O Learn to Take things easily—
Espeshly Other People's Things;
And Time will make your fingers deft
At what is known as Petty Theft.
'Fools and Their Money soon must part!'
And you can help this on, may be,
If, in the kindness of your Heart,
You Learn to Take things easily;
And be, with little education,
A Prince of Misappropriation.
[Pg 92]

V
'A ROLLING STONE GATHERS NO MOSS'

I never understood, I own,
What anybody (with a soul)
Could mean by offering a Stone
This needless warning not to Roll;
And what inducement there can be
To gather Moss, I fail to see.
I'd sooner gather anything,
Like primroses, or news perhaps,
Or even wool (when suffering
A momentary mental lapse);
But could forgo my share of moss,
Nor ever realise the loss.
[Pg 93]
'Tis a botanical disease,
And worthy of remark as such;
Lending a dignity to trees,
To ruins a romantic touch;
A timely adjunct, I've no doubt,
But not worth writing home about.
Of all the Stones I ever met,
In calm repose upon the ground,
I really never found one yet
With a desire to roll around;
Theirs is a stationary rôle.
(A joke,—and feeble on the whole.)
But, if I were a stone, I swear
I'd sooner move and view the World,
Than sit and grow the greenest hair
That ever Nature combed and curled.
I see no single saving grace
In being known as 'Mossyface'!

[Pg 94]
Instead, I might prove useful for
A weapon in the hand of Crime,
A paperweight, a milestone, or
A missile at Election-time;
In each capacity I could
Do quite incalculable good.
When well directed from the Pit,
I might promote a welcome death,
If fortunate enough to hit
Some budding Hamlet or Macbeth,
Who twice each day the playhouse fills,—
(For Further Notice see Small Bills).
At concerts, too, if you prefer,
I could prevent your growing deaf
By silencing the amateur
Before she reached that upper F;
Or else, in lieu of half-a-brick,
Restrain some local Kubelik.
[Pg 95]
Then, human stones, take my advice,
(As you should always do, indeed);
This proverb may be very nice,
But don't you pay it any heed,
And, tho' you make the critics cross,
Roll on, and never mind the moss!
[Pg 96]

VI
'IT IS NEVER TOO LATE TO MEND'

Since it can never be too late
To change your life, or else renew it,
Let the unpleasant process wait,
Until you are *compelled* to do it.
The State provides (and gratis too)
Establishments for such as you.
Remember this, and pluck up heart,
That, be you publican or parson,
Your ev'ry art must have a start,
From petty larceny to arson;
And even in the burglar's trade,
The cracksman is not born, but made.
[Pg 97]
So, if in your career of crime,
You fail to carry out some 'coup,'
Then try again a second time,
And yet again, until you *do*;
And don't despair, or fear the worst,
Because you get found out at first.
Perhaps the battle will not go,
On all occasions, to the strongest;
You may be fairly certain tho'
That He Laughs Last who Laughs the Longest.

So keep a good reserve of laughter,
Which may be found of use hereafter.
Believe me that, howe'er well meant,
A good resolve is always brief;
Don't let your precious hours be spent
In turning over a new leaf.
Such leaves, like Nature's, soon decay,
And then are only in the way.
[Pg 98]
The Road to—well, a certain spot
(A road of very fair dimensions),
Has, so the proverb tells us, got
A parquet-floor of Good Intentions.
Take care, in your desire to please,
You do not add a brick to these.
For there may come a moment when
You shall be mended, willy-nilly,
With many more misguided men,
Whose skill is undermined with skilly.
Till then procrastinate, my friend;
'It *Never* is Too Late to Mend!'
[Pg 99]

VII
'A BAD WORKMAN COMPLAINS OF HIS TOOLS'

This pen of mine is simply grand,
I never loved a pen so much;
This paper (underneath my hand)
Is really a delight to touch;
And never in my life, I think,
Did I make use of finer ink.
The subject upon which I write
Is ev'rything that I could choose;
I seldom knew my wits more bright,
More cosmopolitan my views;
Nor ever did my head contain
So surplus a supply of brain!
[Pg 100]

VIII
'DON'T LOOK A GIFT-HORSE IN THE MOUTH'

I knew a man who lived down South;
He thought this maxim to defy;
He looked a Gift-horse in the Mouth;
The Gift-horse bit him in the Eye!
And, while the steed enjoyed his bite,
My Southern friend mislaid his sight.
Now, had this foolish man, that day,
Observed the Gift-horse in the *Heel*,
It might have kicked his brains away,
But that's a loss he would not feel;
Because, you see (need I explain?),
My Southern friend has got no brain.
[Pg 101]

When any one to you presents
A poodle, or a pocket-knife,
A set of Ping-pong instruments,
A banjo or a lady-wife,
'Tis churlish, as I understand,
To grumble that they're second-hand.
And he who termed Ingratitude
As 'worser nor a servant's tooth'
Was evidently well imbued
With all the elements of Truth;
(While he who said 'Uneasy lies
The tooth that wears a crown' was wise).
'One must be poor,' George Eliot said,
'To know the luxury of giving';
So too one really should be dead
To realise the joy of living.
(I'd sooner be—I don't know which—
I'd *like* to be alive and rich!)
[Pg 102]
This book may be a Gift-horse too,
And one you surely ought to prize;
If so, I beg you, read it through,
With kindly and uncaptious eyes,
Not grumbling because this particular
line doesn't happen to scan,
And this one doesn't rhyme!
[Pg 103]

IX
POTPOURRI

There are many more Maxims to which
I would like to accord a front place,
But alas! I have got
To omit a whole lot,
For the lack of available space;
And the rest I am forced to boil down and condense
To the following Essence of Sound without Sense:
Now the Pitcher that journeys too oft
To the Well will get broken at last.
But you'll find it a fact
That, by using some tact,
Such a danger as this can be past.
[Pg 104] (There's an obvious way, and a simple, you'll own,
Which is, if you're a Pitcher, to Let Well alone.)
Half a loafer is never well-bred,
And Self-Praise is a Dangerous Thing.
And the mice are at play
When the Cat is away,
For a moment, inspecting a King.
(Tho' if Care kills a Cat, as the Proverbs declare,

It is right to suppose that the King will take care.)
Don't Halloo till you're out of the Wood,
When a Stitch in Good Time will save Nine,
While a Bird in the Hand
Is worth Two, understand,
In the Bush that Needs no Good Wine.
(Tho' the two, if they *Can* sing but Won't, have been known,
By an accurate aim to be killed with one Stone.)
[Pg 105]
Never Harness the Cart to the Horse;
Since the latter should be *à la carte*.
Also, Birds of a Feather
Come Flocking Together,
—Because they can't well Flock Apart.
(You may cast any Bread on the Waters, I think,
But, unless I'm mistaken, you can't make it Sink.)
It is only the Fool who remarks
That there Can't be a Fire without Smoke;
Has he never yet learned
How the gas can be turned
On the best incombustible coke?
(Would you value a man by the checks on his suits,
And forget *'que c'est le premier passbook qui Coutts?'*)
Now *'De Mortuis Nil Nisi Bonum,'*
Is Latin, as ev'ry one owns;
If your domicile be
Near a Mortuaree,
[Pg 106] You should always avoid throwing bones.
(I would further remark, if I could,—but I couldn't—
That People Residing in Glasshouses shouldn't.)
You have heard of the Punctual Bird,
Who was First in presenting his Bill;
But I pray you'll be firm,
And remember the Worm
Had to get up much earlier still;
(So that, if you *can't* rise in the morning, then Don't;
And be certain that Where there's a Will there's a Won't.)
You can give a bad name to a Dog,
And hang him by way of excuse;
Whereas Hunger, of course;
Is by far the Best Sauce
For the Gander as well as the Goose.
[Pg 107] (But you shouldn't judge any one just by his looks,
For a Surfeit of Broth ruins too many Cooks.)
With the fact that Necessity knows
Nine Points of the Law, you'll agree.
There are just as Good Fish
To be found on a Dish
As you ever could catch in the Sea.
(You should Look ere you Leap on a Weasel Asleep,
And I've also remarked that Still Daughters Run Cheap.)
The much trodden-on Lane *will* Turn,
And a Friend is in Need of a Friend;
But the Wisest of Saws,
Like the Camel's Last Straws,
Or the Longest of Worms, have an end.
So, before out of Patience a Virtue you make,
A decisive farewell of these maxims we'll take.
[Pg 109]

PART IV
OTHER VERSES
[Pg 111]

BILL
(*Told by the Hospital Orderly*)
At Modder, where I met 'im fust,
I thought as 'ow ole Bill was dead;
A splinter, from a shell wot bust,
'Ad fetched 'im somewheres in the 'ead;
But there! It takes a deal to kill
Them thick-thatched sort o' blokes like Bill.
In the field-'orspital, nex' day,
The doctors was a-makin' out
The 'casualty returns,' an' they
Comes up an' pulls ole Bill about;
Ole Colonel Wilks, 'e turns to me,
'Report this "dangerous,"' sez 'e.
[Pg 112]
But Bill, 'oo must 'ave 'eard it too,
'E calls the doctor, quick as thought:
'I'd take it kindly, sir, if you
'Could keep me out o' the report.
'For tho' I'm 'it, an' 'it severe,
'I doesn't want my friends to 'ear.
'I've a ole mother, 'way in Kent,
''Oo thinks the very world o' me;
'I'd thank you if I wasn't sent
'As "wounded dangerous,"' sez 'e;
'For if she 'ears I'm badly hit,
'I lay she won't get over it.
'At Landman's Drift she lost a lad
'(With the 18th 'Ussars 'e fell),
'Poor soul, she'd take it mighty bad
'To think o' losin' me as well;
'So please, sir, if it's hall the same,
'I'd ask you not to send my name.'
[Pg 113]
The Colonel bloke 'e thinks a bit,
'Oh, well,' sez 'e, 'per'aps you're right.
'And, now I come to look at it,
'I'll send you in as "scalp-wound, slight."
'O' course it's wrong of me, but still—'
'Gawd bless you, sir, an' thanks!' sez Bill.
. . . . . .
'E didn't die; 'e scrambled through.
They hoperated on 'is 'ead,
An' Gawd knows wot they didn't do,—
'Tripoded' 'im, I think they said.
I see'd 'im, Toosday, in Pall Mall,
Nor never knowed 'im look so well.
Yes, Bill 'e's going strong just now,
In London, an' employed again;
Tho' it's a fact, 'e sez, as 'ow
The doctors took out 'alf 'is brain!
Ho well, 'e won't 'ave need o' this—
'E's working at the War Office.
[Pg 114]

THE LEGEND OF THE AUTHOR
(*A long way after Ingoldsby*)
When Anthony Adamson first went to school
The reception he got was decidedly cool;
And, because he was utterly hopeless at games,
He was given all sorts of opprobrious names,
Which ranged the whole gamut from 'fat-head' to 'fool';
For boys as a rule, Are what nurses call 'crool,'
'Tis their natural instinct, which nobody blames,
Any more than the habits Peculiar to rabbits,
To label a duffer 'old woman' or 'muff,' or
Some name calculated to cause him to suffer.
[Pg 115] They failed in their treatment

this time, on the whole,
Since our Anthony thoroughly pitied the rôle
Of the oaf who is muddied, (For Kipling he'd studied),
However strong-hearted, broad-limbed, and warm-blooded,
Who sits in a goal, Quite deficient of soul,
And as blind to the beauties of Life as a mole.
He was rather a curious boy, was this youth,
And a bit of a prig, if you must know the truth,
And his comrades considered him weird and uncouth,
For he didn't much mind When they left him behind,
And, intent upon cricket, Went off to the wicket;
Some other less heating employment he'd find,
And, while his young playfellows fielded and batted,
This curious fat-head, Ink-fingered, hair-matted,
[Pg 116] Would take a new pen from his pocket, and lick it,
Then into the ink-bottle thoughtfully stick it,
And, chewing the holder ('Twas fashioned of gold,
Or at least so 'twas sold By a stationer bold,
And at any rate furnished a good imitation),
In deep rumination, With much mastication,
And wonderful patience, Await inspirations;
And brilliant ideas would arrive on occasions;
When frequently followed, The pen being swallowed,
As up to his eyes in the inkpot he wallowed.
So all the day long and for half of the night
Would young Anthony Adamson nibble and write,
With extravagant feelings of joy and delight,
And it may sound absurd, But 'twas thus, as I've heard,
That he learnt to acquire the appropriate word;
And altho' composition, Which was his ambition,
[Pg 117] At first proved a trifle untamed and refractory;
Arrived in a while At evolving a style
Which a Stevenson even might deem satisfactory.
Now when Anthony A. was as yet in his 'teens
He began to take aim at the big magazines,
With articles, verses, and little love-scenes;
And short stories he wrote, Which he sent with a note
(Which I haven't the space nor the leisure to quote),
Containing a humble request, and a hope,
And some stamps and a clearly addressed envelope.
Now a few of these got to the Editor's desk,
And he found them well-written and quite picturesque,
And he sighed to see talent like this go to waste
On what couldn't appeal to the popular taste.
[Pg 118] For the Public, you see (With a capital P),
Doesn't care what it reads, just so long as it be
Something really exciting, however bad writing,
With wonderful heroes, And villains like Neroes,
Who, running as serials, Wearing imperials,
Revel in bloodshed and bombast and fighting.
So back to the Author his manuscript went;
Altho' sometimes a friendly old Editor sent
An encouraging letter, To say he'd do better
To lower his style to the popular level;
When Anthony proudly (Of course not out loudly,
But mentally) told him to go to the devil!
But a few of his articles never came back,
And their whereabouts no one was able to track,
For some persons who edited, (Can it be credited?)
Finding it paid them, Unduly mislaid them
(Behaviour most rare Nowadays anywhere,
And to ev'ry tradition entirely opposed),
And grew fat on the numerous stamps he enclosed.
[Pg 119] Tho' to this I am really unable to swear,
Or at any rate haven't the courage to dare.
Now when Anthony Adamson grew rather older,
And wiser, and bolder, And broader of shoulder,
He thought he'd a fancy to write for the Press,—
'Tis a common idea with the young, more or less;—
And he saw himself doing Critiques and reviewing
The latest new books as they came from the printers;
To set them on thrones or to smash them to splinters,
To damn with faint praise, Or with eulogies raise,
As he banned or he blest, Just whatever seemed best
To the wit and the wisdom of twenty-three winters.
But when he had carefully read thro' the papers,
Arranged to the taste of our nation of drapers,
[Pg 120] And wisely as Solomon Studied each column, an
Awful attack of despair and depression
Assailed him, and then, As he threw down his pen,
He was forced to confess To no hope of success,
If he entered the great journalistic profession.
For the only description of 'copy' that pays,
In the journals that ev'ry one reads nowadays,
Is the personal matter, Impertinent chat-

ter,
The tales of the tailor, the barber, the hatter;
Society small talk, And mere servants'-hall talk,
The sort of what's-nobody's-business-at-all-talk;
And those who can handle The latest big scandal
With the taste of a Thug and the tact of a Vandal,
Whatever society paper they write in,
Can always provide what their readers delight in.
An article, vulgarly written, which deals
With the food that celebrities eat at their meals
To the popular intellect always appeals.
[Pg 121] People laugh themselves hoarse At the latest divorce,
While a peer's breach of promise is comic, of course;
How eager each face is, As ev'ry one races
To read the details of the Cruelty cases!
And a magistrate's pun Is considered good fun,
And arouses the bench of reporters from torpor,
When it's at the expense of some broken-down pauper!
So Anthony pondered the different ways
Of attaining and gaining the popular praise;
And selected a score of his brightest essays,
Just enough for a book, Which he hopefully took
To some publishers, thinking perhaps they would look
At what might (as he couldn't help modestly hinting)
Repay the expense and the trouble of printing.
[Pg 122] Now the publishers all were extremely polite,
And encouraging quite, For they saw he could write;
But the answer they gave him was always the same.
'You are not,' so they said, 'in the least bit to blame,
And your style is so good, Be it well understood,
We'd be happy to publish your work if we could;
But alas! All the people who know are agreed
This is not what the Public demands, or would read.
'It is over the head Of the people,' they said.
'If you'd only write down to the popular level!'
(Once more, he replied, they could go to the devil!)
The result to our author was not unexpected,
And, as on his failures he sadly reflected,
He took out his pen and a nib he selected,
Then wrote (and his verses Were studded with curses)
This poem, the Lay of the Author (Rejected).
[Pg 123]
The rejected Author's cup
Comes from out a bitter bin,
Constable won't 'take him up,'
Chambers will not 'take him in.'
Publishers, when interviewed,
Each alas! in turn looks Black;
De la Rue is De-la-rude,
Nutt is far too hard to crack.

Author, humble as a vassal
(He is feeling Low as well),
Sadly waits without the Cassell,
Vainly tries to press the Bell.
Author, hourly growing leaner,
Finds each day his jokes more rare,
Asks the Longman if he's Green, or
Spottiswoode to take the Eyre.
[Pg 124]
Author, blithe as lark each morning,
Finds each night his tale unheard,
And, when Fred'rick gives him Warn(e)ing,
Is not Gay as any Bird.
Author, to his writings partial,
Musters their array en bloc,
Which the Simpkins will not Marshall,
And the Elliot will not Stock.
Tho' for little he be yearning,
Yet that little Long he'll want,
When the Lane has got no turning,
And the Richards will not Grant.
Now when Anthony's life it grew harder and harder;
Less coal in the cellar, less meat in the larder;
He thought for a while, And at last (with a smile)
He determined to sacrifice even his style.
[Pg 125] So he wrote just whatever came into his head,
Without any regard for the living or dead,
Or for what his friends thought or his enemies said.
From his style he effaced, As incentives to waste,
All the canons of grammar and even good taste;
And so book after book after book he brought out,
Which you've probably read, and you know all about;
For the publishers bought them, And ev'ry one thought them
So splendidly vulgar, that no one had ever
Read anything quite so improperly clever.
He tried ev'ry style, from the fashion of Ouida's
(His characters being Society Leaders;
The Heroine, suited to middle-class readers,—
A governess she, who might well have been humbler;
The Hero a Duke, an inveterate grumbler;
[Pg 126] And a Guardsman who drank crême-de-menthe from a tumbler)
To that of another more popular lady,
And wrote about aristocrats who were shady,
And showed that the persons you happen to meet
In the Very Best Houses are always effete;
That they gamble all night, in particular sets,
And (Oh, hasn't she said it, Tho' can it be credit-
Ed?) have no intention of paying their debts!
His best, which the Critics said 'teemed with expression,'
Was the one-volume novel 'A Drunkard's Confession';
The next, 'My Good Woman. A Love

Tale'; another,
Most popular this, 'The Flirtations of Mother';
And lastly, the crowning success of his life,
'How the Other Half Lives. By a Baronet's Wife.'
[Pg 127] And the Publishers now are all down on their knees,
As they offer what fees He may happen to please;
And success he discerns As with rapture he learns
The amount that he earns From his roy'lty returns.
(N.B.—I omit the last 'a' here in Royalty,
For reasons of scansion and not from disloyalty.)
The moral of this is quite easy to see;
If a popular author you're anxious to be,
You won't care a digamma For truth or for grammar,
Be far from straitlaced Upon questions of taste,
And don't trouble to polish your style or to bevel,
But always write down to the popular level;
Be vulgar and smart, And you'll get to the heart
Of the persons directing the lit'rary mart,
And your writings must reach (It's a figure of speech)
The—(well, what shall we call it—compositor's) devil!
[Pg 128]

THE MOTRIOT

(*After Robert Browning*)

'It was chickens, chickens, all the way,
With children crossing the road like mad;
Police disguised in the hedgerows lay,
Stop-watches and large white flags they had,
At nine o'clock o' this very day.
'I broke the record to Tunbridge Wells,
And I shouted aloud, to all concerned,
"Give room, good folk, do you hear my bells?"
But my motor skidded and overturned;
Then exploded—and afterwards, what smells!
[Pg 129]
'Alack! it was I rode over the son
Of a butcher; rolled him all of a heap!
Nought man could do did I leave undone;
And I thought that butcher's boys were cheap,—
But this, poor man, 'twas his only one.
'There's nobody in my motor now,—
Just a tangled car in the ditch upset;
For the fun of the fair is, all allow,
At the County Court, or, better yet,
By the very foot of the dock, I trow.
. . . . .
'Thus I entered, and thus I go;
In Court the magistrate sternly said,
"Five guineas fine, and the costs you owe!"
I might not question, so promptly paid.
Henceforth I *walk*; I am safer so.'
[Pg 130]

THE BALLAD OF THE ARTIST

Archibald Ames is an artist,
And a widely renowned R.A.,
For albeit his pictures are thoroughly bad,
The greatest success he has always had,
And he makes his profession pay.
He has no idea of proportion,
No notion of colour or line,
But perhaps for such there is little need,
Since everybody is fully agreed
That his *subjects* are quite divine.
[Pg 131]
His pictures are sweetly simple;
The ingredients all must know,—
Just a fair-haired child and a dog or two,
A very old man, and a baby's shoe,
And some bunches of mistletoe.
In some, an angelic infant
Is helping a kitten to play,
Or dressing a cat in Grandpapa's hat
(Which is equally hard on the hat and the cat),
Or teaching a 'dolly' to pray.
Or else there's a runaway couple,
With a distant view of papa,
An elderly party with rich man's gout,
Who swears himself rapidly inside out,
In a broken-down motor-car.
Or it may be a scene in the Workhouse,
Where a widow of high degree,
[Pg 132] With almost suspiciously puce-coloured hair,
Has arrived in a gorgeous carriage-and-pair,
To distribute a pound of tea.
Sometimes he portrays a battle,
With a 'square' like a Rugby scrum,
Where a bugler, the colours grasped in his hand,
And making a final determined stand,
Plays 'God Save the King' on a drum.
This is the kind of subject
That he gives to us day by day;
You may jeer at the absence of all technique,
But these are the pictures the people seek
From this justly renowned R.A.
In distant suburban boudoirs
You will find them, in gilded frames,
'The Prodigal Calf' (a homely scene)
'Grandmamma's Boots,' or 'To Gretna Green,'
The Works of Archibald Ames.
[Pg 133]
And, if they appeal to the public,
In the usual course of events,
Some enterprising manager comes,
And buys them up for enormous sums,
And they serve as advertisements.
Where the child is painting the kitten
With Potter's Indelible Dye,
While Grandpapa shows to the reckless cat
McBride's Indestructible Gibus Hat,
(Which Ev'ry one ought to buy).
And the Gretna Green arrangement
An interest new acquires,
By depicting how great the advantages are
Of the Patented Spoofenhauss Auto-car,
With unpuncturable tyres.
And the widow (Try Kay's for mourning),
As black as Stevenson's Ink,
[Pg 134] Is curing the paupers of sundry ills
By the gift of a box of the Palest Pills
For persons who may be Pink.
And the bugler-boy in the battle,
With trousers of Blackett's Blue,
Unshrinking as Simpson's Serge, and free
As Winkleson's Patent Ear-drum he,
And steadfast as Holdhard's Glue.
This is the modern fashion
In the popular art of the day,
And this is the reason that Archibald Ames

Ranks high among other familiar names
As a very well-known R.A.
[Pg 135]

THE BALLAD OF PING-PONG
(After Swinburne)

The murmurous moments of May-time,
What bountiful blessings they bring!
As dew to the dawn of the day-time,
Suspicions of Summer to Spring!
Let others imagine the time light,
With maidens or books on their knee,
Or live in the languorous limelight
That tinges the trunk of the Tree.
[Pg 136]
Let the timorous turn to their tennis,
Or the bowls to which bumpkins belong,
But the thing for grown women and men is
The pastime of ping and of pong.
The game of the glorious glamour!
The feeling to fight till you fall!
The hurricane hail and the hammer!
The batter and bruise of the ball!
The glory of getting behind it!
The brief but bewildering bliss!
The fear of the failure to find it!
The madness at making a miss!
The sound of the sphere as you smack it,
Derisive, decisive, divine!
The riotous rush of your racket,
To mix and to mingle with mine!
[Pg 137]
The diadem dear to the King is,
How sweet to the singer his song;
To me so the plea of the ping is,
And the passionate plaint of the pong.
I live for it, love for it, like it;
Delight of my dearest of dreams!
To stand and to strive and to strike it,—
So certain, so simple it seems!
Then give me the game of the gay time,
The ball on its wandering wing,
The pastime for night or for day-time,
The Pong, not to mention the Ping!
[Pg 138]

THE PESSIMIST
(After Maeterlinck)

Life's bed is full of crumbs and rice,
No roses float on my lagoon;
There are no fingers, white and nice,
To rub my head with scented ice,
Or feed me with a spoon.
I think of all the days gone by,
Replete with black and blue regret;
No comets light my glaucous sky,
My tears are hardly ever dry,
I never can forget!
[Pg 139]
I see the yellow dog, Desire,
That strains against the lead of Hope,
With lilac eyes and lips of fire,
As all in vain he strives to tire
The hand that holds the rope.
I see the kisses of the past,
Like lambkins dying in the snow,
The honeymoon that did not last,
The tinted youth that flew so fast,
And all this vale of woe.
So, raising high my raucous cry,
I ask (and Fates no answer give),
Why am I pre-ordained to die?
O cruel Fortune, tell me, why
Am I allowed to live?
[Pg 140]

THE PLACE WHERE THE OLD CLEEK BROKE
(After Whyte-Melville)

Life is hollow to the golfer, of however high his rank,
If the dock-leaf and the nettle grow too free,
If a bramble bar his progress, if he's bunkered by a bank,
If his golf-ball jerks and wobbles off the tee.
There's a ditch I never pass, full of stones and broken glass,
And I'd sooner lift my ball and count a stroke,
For the tears my vision blot when I see the fatal spot,
'Tis the place where my old cleek broke.
[Pg 141]
There's his haft upon the table, there's his head upon a chair;
And a better never felt the summer rain;
I may curse and I may swear, my umbrella-stand is bare,
I shall never use my gallant cleek again!
With what unaccustomed speed would he strike the Golf-ball teed!
How it sounded on his metal at each stroke!
Not a flyer in the game such parabolas could claim,
At the place where the old cleek broke!
Was he cracked? I hardly think it. Did he slip? I do not know.
He had struck the ball for forty yards or more;
He was driving smooth and even, just as hard as he could go,
I had never seen him striking so before.
[Pg 142] But I hardly can complain, for there must have been a strain
I had forced beyond the compass of a joke—
And no club, however strong, could have lasted over long
At the place where the old cleek broke!
There are men, both staid and sound, who hold it happiness unique,
At which only the irreverent can scoff,
That is reached by means of brassey, driver, niblick, spoon, or cleek,
And that life is not worth living without Golf.
Well, I hope it may be so; for myself I only know
That I never more shall try another stroke;
Yes, I've wearied of the sport, since a lesson I was taught,
At the place where the old cleek broke.
[Pg 143]

THE HOMES OF LONDON
(After Mrs. Hemans)

The happy homes of London,
How beautiful they stand!
The crowded human rookeries
That mar this Christian land.
Where cats in hordes upon the roof
For nightly music meet,
And the horse, with non-adhesive hoof,
Skates slowly down the street.
The merry homes of London!
Around bare hearths at night,
With hungry looks and sickly mien,
The children wail and fight.
[Pg 144] There woman's voice is only heard
In shrill, abusive key,
And men can hardly speak a word
That is not blasphemy.
The healthy homes of London!
With weekly wifely wage,
The hopeless husbands, out of work,
Their daily thirst assuage.
The overcrowded tenement
Is comfortless and bare,
The atmosphere is redolent

Of hunger and despair.
The blessed homes of London!
By thousands, on her stones,
The helpless, homeless, destitute,
Do nightly rest their bones.
[Pg 145] On pavements Piccadilly way,
In slumber like the dead,
Their wan pathetic forms they lay,
And make their humble bed.
The free, fair homes of London!
From all the thinking throng,
Who mourn a nation's apathy,
The cry goes up, 'How long!'
And those who love old England's name,
Her welfare and renown,
Can only contemplate with shame
The homes of London town.
[Pg 146]

THE HAPPIEST LAND

(After Longfellow)
There sat one day in a tavern,
Somewhere near Lincoln's Inn,
Six sleepy-looking working men,
Imbibing 'twos' of gin.
The Potman filled their tankards
With the liquor each preferred,
Torpid and somnolent they sat,
And spake not one rude word.
But when the potman vanished,
A brawny Scot stood forth;
'Change here,' quoth he, 'for Aberdeen,
Strathpeffer and the North!
[Pg 147]
'No country in the world, I ken,
With Scotia can compare,
With all the dour and canny men,
And the bonnie lasses there.
'I hae a wee bit hoosie,
An' a burn runs greetin' by,
An' unco crockit Minister
An' a bairn to milk the ki';
'I hae a muckle haggis,
A bap an' a skian-dhu,
A cairngorm and a bannock,
An' a sonsy kailyard too!'
'Bejabers!' said an Irishman,
'Acushla and Ochone!
There's but one country on the Earth,
Ould Oireland stands alone!
[Pg 148]
'Give me the Emerald Isle, avick!
With murphies for to ate,
An' as many pigs and childer
As the fingers on me *fate*.'

Exclaimed a Frenchman, 'Par Exemple!
Donnez-moi ma Patrie!
Vin ordinaire and savoir faire
Are good enough for me!
'Have you the penknife of my Aunt?
Mais non, hélas! but then,
The female gardener has got
Some paper and a pen!'
Then spoke a Greek, 'The Isles of Greece!
What can compare with those?
Thalassa! and Eurêka!
Rhodódaktylos êôs!'
[Pg 149]
'On London streets I'm working,
With a vat of asphalt stew,
Putting off the old macadam,
And a-laying down the new;
'But the country of my childhood
Is the best that man may know,
Oh didêmi also phêmi,
Zôê mou sas agapô!'
Straight rose a German and remarked
'Vot of die Vaterland?
Ach Himmel! Unberüfen!
And the luffly German band?
'Gif me some Gotterdammerung,
And nuddings more I need,
But ewigkeit and sauerkraut
And niebelungenlied!'
[Pg 150]
'Nonsense!' exclaimed an Englishman.
('I surely ought to know!')
Old England is the only place
Where any man should go!
'Show me the something furriner
Who such a fact denies,
And, if I can't convince 'im,
I can black 'is bloomin' eyes!'
Then entered in the potman,
And pointed to the door;
'Outside,' said he, 'is where *you*'ll go,
If I have any more!'
. . . . .
It was six friendly working men,
Brimming with 'twos' of gin,
Who crept from out the tavern,
As the Dawn came creeping in.
[Pg 151]

A LONDON INVOLUNTARY

(After W. E. Henley)
   Spizzicato non poco skirtsando
Old Palace Yard!
Hark how their breath draws lank and hard,
The sallow stern police!
Breaking the desultory midnight peace
With plangent call, to cry
'Division'! This their first especial charge.
And now, low, luminous, and large,
The slumbrous Member hurries by.
Let us take cab, Dear Heart, take cab and go
From out the lith of this loud world (I know
[Pg 152] The meaning of the word).
Come, let us hie
To where the lamp-posts ouch the troubled sky,—
(And if there is one thing for which I vouch
It is my knowledge of the verb to ouch.)
So, as we steal
Homeward together, we shall feel
The buxom breeze,—
(Observe the epithet; an apt one, if you please.)
Down through the sober paven street,
Which, purged and sweet,
Gleams in the ambient deluge of the water-cart,
Bemused and blurred and pinkly lustrous, where
The blandest lion in Trafalgar Square
Seems but a part
Of the great continent of light,—
An attribute of the embittered night,—
How new, how naked and how clean!
Couchant, slow, shimmering, superb!
Constant to one environment, nor even seen
Pottering aimlessly along the kerb.
[Pg 153] Lo!
On the pavement, one of those
Grim men who go down to the sea in ships,
Blaspheming, reeling in a foul ellipse,
Home to some tangled alley-bedside goes,—
Oozing and flushed, sharing his elemental mirth
With all the jocund undissembling earth;
Drooping his shameless nose,
Nor hitching up his drifting, shifting clothes.
And here is Piccadilly! Loudly dense,
Intractable, voluminous, immense!
(Dear, dear my heart's desire, can I be

talking sense?)
[Pg 154]

BLUEBEARD

Yes, I am Bluebeard, and my name
Is one that children cannot stand;
Yet once I used to be so tame
I'd eat out of a person's hand;
So gentle was I wont to be,
A Curate might have played with me.
People accord me little praise,
Yet I am not the least alarming;
I can recall, in bygone days,
A maid once said she thought me charming.
She was my friend,—no more I vow,—
And—she's in an asylum now.
[Pg 155]
Girls used to clamour for my hand,
Girls I refused in simple dozens;
I said I'd be their brother, and
They promised they would be my cousins.
(One I accepted,—more or less,—
But I've forgotten her address.)
They worried me like anything
By their proposals ev'ry day;
Until at last I had to ring
The bell, and have them cleared away;
They longed to share my lofty rank,
Also my balance at the bank.
My hospitality to those
Whom I invite to come and stay
Is famed; my wine like water flows,—
Exactly like, some people say;
But this is mere impertinence
To one who never spares expense.
[Pg 156]
When through the streets I walk about,
My subjects stand and kiss their hands,
Raise a refined metallic shout,
Wave flags and warble tunes on bands;
While bunting hangs on ev'ry front,—
With my commands to let it bunt!
When I come home again, of course,
Retainers are employed to cheer,
My paid domestics get quite hoarse
Acclaiming me, and you can hear
The welkin ringing to the sky,—
Ay, ay, and let it welk, say I!
And yet, in spite of this, there are
Some persons who, at diff'rent times,
—(Because I am so popular)—
Accuse me of most awful crimes;
A girl once said I was a flirt!
Oh my! how the expression hurt!

[Pg 157]
I *never* flirted in the least,
Never for very long, I mean,—
Ask any lady (now deceased)
Who partner of my life has been;—
Oh well, of course, sometimes, perhaps,
I meet a girl, like other chaps,—
And, if I like her very much,
And if she cares for me a bit,
Where is the harm of look or touch,
If neither of us mentions it?
It isn't right, I don't suppose,
But no one's hurt if no one knows!
One should not break oneself *too* fast
Of little habits of this sort,
Which may be definitely classed
With gambling, or a taste for port;
They should be *slowly* dropped, until
The Heart is subject to the Will.
[Pg 158]
I knew a man (in Regent Street)
Who, at a very slight expense,
By persevering, was complete-
Ly cured of Total Abstinence
An altered life he has begun
And takes a glass with any one.
I knew another man, whose wife
Was an invet'rate suicide;
She daily strove to take her life,
And (naturally) nearly died;
But some such system she essayed,
And now—she's eighty in the shade.
Ah, the new leaves I try to turn!
But, like so many men in town,
I seem (as with regret I learn)
Merely to turn the corner down;
A habit which, I fear, alack!
Makes it more easy to turn back.
[Pg 159]
I have been criticised a lot;
I venture to inquire what for?
Because, forsooth, I have not got
The instincts of a bachelor!
Just hear my story, you will find
How grossly I have been maligned.
I was unlucky with my wives,
So are the most of married men;
Undoubtedly they lost their lives,—
Of course, but even so, what then?
I loved them like no other man,
And I *can* love, you bet I can!
My first was little Emmeline,
More beautiful than day was she;
Her proud, aristocratic mien
Was what at once attracted me.

I naturally did not know
That I should soon dislike her so.
[Pg 160]
But there it was! And you'll infer
I had not very long to wait
Before my red-hot love for her
Turned to unutterable hate.
So, when this state of things I found,
I had her casually drowned.
My next was Sarah, sweet but shy,
And quite inordinately meek;
Yes, even now I wonder why
I had her hanged within the week;
Perhaps I felt a bit upset,
Or else she bored me. I forget.
Then came Evangeline, my third,
And when I chanced to be away,
She, so I subsequently heard,
Was wont (I deeply grieve to say)
With my small retinue to flirt.
I strangled her. I hope it hurt.
[Pg 161]
Isabel was, I think, my next,—
(That is, if I remember right),—
And I was really very vexed
To find her hair come off at night;
To falsehood I could not connive,
And so I had her boiled alive.
Then came Sophia, I believe,
Her coiffure was at least her own;
Alas! she fancied to deceive
Her friends, by altering its tone.
She dyed her locks a flaming red!
I suffocated her in bed.
Susannah Maud was number six,
But she did not survive a day;
Poor Sue, she had no parlour tricks,
And hardly anything to say.
A little strychnine in her tea
Finished her off, and I was free.
[Pg 162]
Yet I did not despair, and soon,
In spite of failures, started off
Upon my seventh honeymoon,
With Jane; but could not stand her cough.
'Twas chronic. Kindness was in vain.
I pushed her underneath the train.
Well, after her, I married Kate,
A most unpleasant woman. Oh!
I caught her at the garden gate,
Kissing a man I didn't know;
And, as that didn't suit me quite,
I blew her up with dynamite.
Most married men, so sorely tried

As this, would have been rather bored.
Not I, but chose another bride,
And married Ruth. Alas! she snored!
I served her just the same as Kate,
And so she joined the other eight.
[Pg 163]
My last was Grace; I am not clear,
I *think* she didn't like me much;
She used to scream when I came near,
And shuddered at my lightest touch.
She seemed to wish to keep aloof,
And so I threw her off the roof.
This is the point I wish to make;—
From all the wives for whom I grieve,
Whose lives I had perforce to take,
Not one complaint did I receive;
And no expense was spared to please
My spouses at their obsequies.
My habits, I would have you know,
Are perfect, as they've always been;
You ask if I am good, and go
To church, and keep my fingers clean?
I do, I mean to say I am,
I have the morals of a lamb.
[Pg 164]
In my domains there is no sin,
Virtue is rampant all the time,
Since I so thoughtfully brought in
A bill which legalises crime;
Committing things that are not wrong
Must pall before so very long.
And if what you imagine vice
Is not considered so at all,
Crime doesn't seem the least bit nice,
There's no temptation then to fall;
For half the charm of things we do
Is knowing that we oughtn't to.
Believe me, then, I am not bad,
Though in my youth I had to trek,
Because I happened to have had
Some difficulties with a cheque.
What forgery in some might be
Is absent-mindedness in me!
[Pg 165]
I know that I was much abused,
No doubt when I was young and rash,
But I should not have been accused
Of misappropriating cash.
I may have sneaked a silver dish;—
Well, you may search me if you wish!
So, now you see me, more or less,
As I would figure in your thoughts;
A trifle given to excess,
And prone perhaps to vice of sorts;
When tempted, rather apt to fall,
But still—a good chap after all!
[Pg 166]

'THE WOMAN WITH THE DEAD SOLES'

(*After Stephen Phillips*)
Attracted to the frozen river's brink,
Where on a small impromptu snow-swept rink,
The happy skaters darted left and right,
Or circled amorously out of sight,
Some self-supporting; some, like falling stars,
Spread-eagling ankle-weak parabolas;
I watched the human swarm, and I was 'ware
A woman, disarranged, knelt on a chair.
She had cold feet on which she could not run,
And piteously she thawed them in the sun.
[Pg 167] Those feet were of a woman that alone
Was kneeling; a pink liquid by her shone,
Which raising to her luminous, lantern jaw,
She sipped; or idly stirred it with a straw.
Upon her hat she wore a kind of fowl,
An hummingbird, I ween, or else an owl.
Then turned to me. I looked the other way,
Trembling; I knew the words she wished to say.
So warm her gaze the blood rushed to my head,
Instinctively I knew her feet were dead.
Amorphous feet, like monumental moons,
Pavement-obliterating, vast, pontoons,
Superbly varnished, to the ice had come,
And now, snow-kissed, frost-fettered, dangled numb.
Gently she spoke,—the while my senses whirled,
Of 'largest circulations in the world';
Wildly she spoke, as babble men in dreams,
Of feeling life's blood 'rushing to extremes';
But I ignored her with deliberate stare,
[Pg 168] Until the indelicate thing began to swear.
Sensations as of pins and needles rose,
Apollinaris-like, in tingled toes.
She felt the hungry frost that punctured holes,
Like concentrated seidlitz, in her soles.
Feebly she stept; and sudden was aware
Her feet had gone,—they were no longer there,—
And from her boots was willing to be freed;
She would not keep what she could never need.
Sullenly I consented, and withdrew
From either heel a huge chaotic shoe;
Yet for a time laboriously and slow
She journeyed with her ponderous boots, as though
Along with her she could not help but bear
The bargelike burdens she was wont to wear.
Towards me she reeled; and 'Oh! my Uncle,' cried,
'My Uncle!' but I pushed her to one side,
Then smiled upon her so she could not stay,—
(My smile can frighten motor-cars away):—
[Pg 169] While thus I grinned, not knowing what to do,
A belted beadle, in immaculate blue,
Plucked at my sleeve, and shattered my romance,
Wheeling on cushion tires an ambulance.
Deliberately then he laid her there,
Tucked in and bore away; I did not care!
[Pg 170]

ROSEMARY

(*A Ballad of the Boudoir*)
'E'er August be turned to September,
Nor Summer to Autumn as yet,
My darling, you Autumn remember
What Summer so sure to forget.
'Though age may extinguish the ember
That glowed in our hearts when we met,
Remember, my love, to remember,
And I will forget to forget.
'Who knows but the winds of December
May drift us asunder, my pet;
And if I forget to remember,
Remember, my sweet, to forget!
[Pg 171]
'My beauty will fade, as the posy

You gave me that night on the stairs;
My lips will not always be rosy,
My head cannot give itself 'airs.
'Alas! as we both become older,
Existence draws nigh to a close;
So, until I've forgotten your shoulder,
You must not remember my nose.
'Our days were not all sunny weather;
Even so we have nought to regret,—
Ah! let us remember together,
Until we forget to forget!'
[Pg 172]

PORTKNOCKIE'S PORTER

(*With apologies to Porphyria's Lover*)
The train came early in to-night,
The sullen guard was soon awake,
And threw my luggage down, for spite,
To where the platform seemed a lake;
And did his best my box to break.
When sidled up a porter; straight,
He mopped the platform with a broom,
And, kneeling, made the well-filled grate
Blaze up within the waiting-room,
And so dispelled the usual gloom.
Which done, he came and took his seat
Beside me, doffed his coat, untied
His bootlaces, and let his feet
[Pg 173] Peep coyly out on either side;
Then called me. When no voice replied,
He rolled his shirt-sleeve up, and rose,
And laid his brawny biceps bare,
And, where my eyebrows meet my nose,
He slowly shook his fist, just there,
And seized me by my yellow hair.
Then roughly asked me, had I got
A head as empty as a bubble?
Bidding me sternly, did I not
Desire henceforth to see things double,
To give him something for his trouble.
Nor could my arguments prevail;
Entreaties, threats were all in vain!
Returned he to the twice-told tale
Of how, from out the midnight train,
He bore my luggage through the rain.
I fixed him with my cold grey eye,
But all in vain; at last I knew
That porter hated me; (though why
[Pg 174] I cannot understand, can you?)
And what on earth was I to do!
Next moment, though I still perspire
To think of it, I quickly found
A thing to do; and on the fire
I pushed him backwards with a bound,
And piled the coal up all around.
Cremated him. No pain he felt.
As a shut coop that holds a hen,
I oped the register and smelt
An odour as of burnt quill-pen.
My laughter bubbled over then.
I seized him lightly, with the tongs
About his waist; and through the door
I bore him, burning with my wrongs,
And laid him on the line. What's more,
The down express was due at four.
. . . . .
The mark is on the metals still,
A gruesome stain, I must confess,
[Pg 175] And, when I pass, it makes me ill
To note the somewhat painful mess
Concocted by the down express.
Portknockie's porter; so he died.
The date of inquest is deferred.
'Tis thought a case of suicide;
And he who might have seen or heard,—
The guard,—has never said a word.
[Pg 176]

THE BALLAD OF THE LITTLE JINGLANDER

'WHEN THE MOTHER COUNTRY CALLS!'
(*With apologies to all concerned*)
North and South and East and West, the message travels fast!
East and West and North and South, the bugles blare and blast!
North and West and East and South, the battle-cry grows plain!
West and South and North and East, it echoes back again!
[Pg 177]
For the East is calling Westwards, and the North is speaking South,
There's a threat on ev'ry curling lip, an oath in ev'ry mouth;
'Tis the shadow of an Empire o'er the Universe that falls,
And the winds of Heaven wonder when the Mother-country calls!
Now the call is carried coastwise, from Calay to Bungapore,
From the sunny South Pacific to the North Atlantic shore;
Gathers volume in its footsteps and grows grander as it goes,
From Jeboom to Pongawongo, where the Rumtumpootra flows.
The 'native-born' he sits alert beneath a deodar,
He sharpens up his 'cummerbund' and loads his 'khitmagar,'
[Pg 178]
His 'ekkah' stands untasted, as he girds upon his brow
The 'syce' his father gave him, saying 'unkah punkah jow!'
Come forth, you babu jemadar,
No lackh of pice we bring,
Bid the ferash comb your moustashe,
And join the great White King!
And Westward, where 'Our Lady of the Sunshine' (not 'the Snows')
Delights to herd the caribou, and where the chipmunk grows,
The 'habitant' he sits amid a grove of maple trees,
He decorates his shanty and he polishes his 'skis.'
And see! Through ranch or lumber-camp, where'er the news shall go,
The daughters cease to gather fruit, the sons to shovel snow!
[Pg 179]
They love the dear old Mother-land that they have never seen,
The Empire that they advertise as 'vaster than has been'!
Come forth, you mild militiaman,
To conquer or to fail,
Who is it helps the Lion's whelps
Untwist the Lion's tail?
The pride of race, the pride of place, and bond of blood they feel,
The Indies indicate it and New Zealand shows new zeal.
The daughters in their Mother's house are mistress in their own;
They are her heirs, her flesh is theirs, and they would share her bone!
Lo! Greater Britain stretches out her hands across the sea;
Australia forgets her impecuniositee;
[Pg 180] On Afric's shore the wily Boer is ready now to fight,
For the Khaki and the rooinek, for the Empire and the Right!
Come forth, you valiant volunteer,
Come forth to do or die,
You give a hand to Mother, and
She'll help you by and by!
Upon her score of distant shores the sun

is always bright;
(And always in her empire, too, it must somewhere be night!)
Her birthplace is the Ocean, where her pennon braves the breeze;
Her motto, 'What is ours we'll hold (and what is not we'll seize!)'
Her rule is strong, her purse is long, her sons are stern and true,
[Pg 181] With iron hands she holds her lands (and other people's too).
She sees her chance and cries 'Advance,' while others stand and gape,
Her oxengoads shall claim the roads from Cairo to the Cape.
Come out, you big black Fuzzy-Wuz,
You've got to take your share;
We'll make you sweat till you forget
You broke a British Square!
North and South and East and West, the message travels fast!
East and West and North and South, the bugles blare and blast!
Hear we but a whisper that the foe is at the walls,
And, by Gad, we'll show them something when the Mother Country calls!
[Pg 182]

AFTWORD

'Tis done! We reach the final page
With feelings of relief, I'm certain;
And there arrives, at such a stage,
The moment to ring down the Curtain.
(This metaphor is freely taken
From Shakespeare,—or perhaps from Bacon.)
The Book perused, our Future brings
A plethora of blank to-morrows,
When memories of Happier Things
Will be our Sorrow's Crown of Sorrows.
(I trust you recognise this line
As being Tennyson's, not mine.)
[Pg 183]
My verses may indeed be few,
But are they not, to quote the poet,
'The sweetest things that ever grew
Beside a human door'? I know it!
(What an *in*human door would be,
Enquire of Wordsworth, please, not me.)
'Twas one of my most cherished dreams
To write a Moral Book some day;—
What says the Bard? 'The best laid schemes
Of Mice and Men gang aft agley!'
(The Bard here mentioned, by the bye,
Is Robbie Burns, of course,—not I.)
And tho' my pen records each thought
As swift as the phonetic Pitman,
Morality is not my 'forte,'
O Camarados! (*vide* Whitman).
And, like the Porcupine, I still
Am forced to ply a fretful quill.
[Pg 184]
We may be Masters of our Fate,
(As Henley was inspired to mention),
Yet am I but the Second Mate
Upon the s.s. 'Good Intention';
For me the course direct is lacking,—
I have to do a deal of tacking.
To seek for Morals here's a task
Of which you well may be despairing;
'What has become of them?' you ask.
They've given me the slip,—like Waring.
'Look East!' said Browning once, and I
Would make a similar reply.
Look East, where in a garret drear,
The Author works, without cessation,
Composing verses for a mere-
Ly nominal remuneration;
And, while he has the strength to write 'em,
Will do so still—*ad infinitum!*
[Pg 185]

ENVOI

Speed, flippant rhymes, throughout the land;
Disperse yourselves with patient zeal!
Go, perch upon the critic's hand,
Just after he has had a meal.
But should he still unfriendly be,
Unperch and hasten back to me.
. . . . .
O gentle maid, O happy boy,
This copy of my book is done;
But don't forget that I enjoy
A royalty on ev'ry one;
Just think how wealthy I should be,
If you would purchase two or three!
[Pg 186]

MORAL

No moral that I ever took
Seemed quite so evident before.
If purchasing an author's book
Will keep the wolf from his back-door,
It is our very obvious mission
To buy up the entire edition.
FINIS.

Printed by T. and A. Constable, Printers to His Majesty at the Edinburgh University Press

BY THE SAME AUTHOR.

Fiscal Ballads.

(Second Impression.)
Fcap. 8vo. 1s. net.

'The fiscal controversy has not been very fruitful in verse. So far as we are aware, only one balladist has found any genuine inspiration in it. That is Mr. Harry Graham, whose skill as a rhymer in other directions has already been abundantly proved. The ballads for the most part take a colloquial form, and while containing much humour, are full of sound doctrine. Mr. Graham, it will be seen, has great facility in rhyme, and in all this rhyme there is reason. When the General Election comes this book should be a gold-mine for the political reciter.'—*Westminster Gazette.*

'A most amusing contribution to the literature of the fiscal controversy.'—*Daily Telegraph.*

'True ballads, with abundant vigour and piquancy.'—*Aberdeen Free Press.*

'Good both in intention and execution.'—*Speaker.*

'These ballads . are very good. Indeed, we cannot remember any recent example of political truths expressed with such exactness as well as spirit in humorous verse. The fun is as good as the argument. Of this admirable little book we will only say, in conclusion, that it will amuse and delight even those who had imagined that nothing more worth reading could possibly be printed on the fiscal question. We would strongly urge such persons to invest a shilling in "Fiscal Ballads," for we are confident they will not be disappointed. If the Free-Trade organisations are wise, they will seek leave to reprint selections from them in leaflets which can be circulated by the million.'—*Spectator.*

LONDON: EDWARD ARNOLD, 41 & 43 Maddox St., W.

Ruthless Rhymes for Heartless Homes.

Illustrated by 'G. H.'

Oblong 4to. 3s. 6d.

'It is impossible not to be amused by some of the "Ruthless Rhymes for Heartless Homes," by Colonel D. Streamer, nor can any one with a sense of humour fail to appreciate the many amusing points in the illustrations.'—*Westminster.*

'"Ruthless Rhymes for Heartless Homes" is the name of a really charming little book of rhymes. The words are by Col. D. Streamer, and the illustrations by "G. H.," and 'tis hard to say whether words or pictures are the cleverer. The book is one which must, however, be seen to be appreciated; to properly describe it is impossible.'—*Calcutta Englishman.*

'Wise parents will, however, keep strictly to themselves "Ruthless Rhymes for Heartless Homes," by Col. D. Streamer. The illustrations by "G. H." are very amusing, and especially happy is that to "Equanimity," when
"Aunt Jane observed the second time
She tumbled off a 'bus,
The step is short from the sublime
To the ridiculous."'
—*Daily Telegraph.*

'Another charming whimsicality published by Mr. Edward Arnold is "Ruthless Rhymes for Heartless Homes."'—*Sydney Morning Herald.*

'The veriest nonsense, possessing the quality that makes it akin to Carroll's work.'—*New York Bookworm.*

'It is difficult to see the humour of
"Philip, foozling with his cleek,
Drove his ball through Helen's cheek.
Sad they bore her corpse away,
Seven up and six to play."'
—*Scotsman.*

LONDON: EDWARD ARNOLD, 41 & 43 Maddox St., W.

Ballads of the Boer War.

Fcap. 8vo, buckram. 3s. 6d. net.
(Second Edition.)

'There is unquestionably a good deal of human nature in the book, and as an expression of sentiments which have remained hitherto inarticulate, as a revelation not always edifying, but often illuminating, of the heart of the man in the ranks, this little volume is a distinct addition to the literature of the war.'—*Spectator.*

'Racy expressions of Tommy Atkins' feelings in Tommy Atkins' language. "Coldstreamer's" verses in their kind are as good as any we have seen.'—*Academy.*

'These colloquial rhymes express the private soldier's views in his own language.'—*The Times.*

'These racy ballads make a book which many will read with interest and sympathy.'—*Scotsman.*

'As good as anything yet done in the vernacular of Mr. Thomas Atkins. A book for every friend of the army.'—*Outlook.*

'One of the liveliest books of light verse we have come across for a long time.'—*County Gentleman.*

'Vigorous Kiplingesque verses, with sound common-sense and genuine feeling. Well worth reading and buying.'—*To-Day.*

'Mephitic exhalations.'—*Daily News.*

LONDON: GRANT RICHARDS, 48 Leicester Square, W.C.

Misrepresentative Men.

Illustrated by F. STROTHMAN.
(*Second Edition.*)
OPINIONS OF THE AMERICAN PRESS.

'One of the most amusing books of the year. Mr. Graham is a fluent and ingenious rhymester, with an alert mind and a well-controlled sense of humour.'—*The Times* (New York).

'"Misrepresentative Men" shows so high-spirited a mastery of words and metre (the result, we take it, of laborious days) that it will be read with pleasure by the most fastidious lover of what is amusing.'—*The Nation* (New York).

'Mr. Graham's verses are exceedingly clever, and Mr. Strothman's illustrations add to their cleverness.'—*The Bookman* (New York).

'A very amusing little book, by that cleverly humorous versifier "Col. D. Streamer," whose *Ruthless Rhymes for Heartless Homes* has had such a deserved vogue.'—*Town Topics* (New York).

'The most amusing biographical caricatures of celebrities that we have read for a long time. There is not a dull line in the entire collection.'—*The Bookseller* (New York).

'These satirical verses have the same ingenious humour as the writer's previous rhymes. The book is altogether refreshing.'—*Town and Country* (New York).

'The hit of the season.'—*The Lexington Herald.*

'A most attractively humorous work.'—*The Pittsburg Despatch.*

'A little book of really clever verse.'—*The Milwaukee Sentinel.*

LONDON: GAY AND BIRD, 22 Bedford Street, Strand .

SELECTIONS FROM MR. EDWARD ARNOLD'S LIST OF NEW AND RECENT BOOKS.

THE LIFE AND TIMES OF THE RIGHT HON. CECIL JOHN RHODES.

By the HON. SIR LEWIS MICHELL. *Illustrated. Two volumes, demy 8vo.,* 30s. net.

This important work will take rank as the authoritative biography of one of the greatest of modern Englishmen. Sir Lewis Michell, who has been engaged upon the work for five years, is an executor of Mr. Rhodes' will, and a trustee of the Rhodes Estate. He was an intimate personal friend of Mr. Rhodes for many years, and has had access to all the papers at Groote Schuur. Hitherto, although many partial appreciations of the great man have been published in the Press or in small volumes, no complete and well-informed life of him has appeared. The gap has now been filled by Sir Lewis Michell so thoroughly that we have in these two volumes what will undoubtedly be the final estimate of Mr. Rhodes' career for many years to come.

THE REMINISCENCES OF ADMIRAL MONTAGU.

With Illustrations. One volume, demy 8vo., cloth, 15s. net.

The Author of this entertaining book, Admiral the Hon. Victor Montagu, has passed a long life divided between the amusements of aristocratic society in this country and the duties of naval service afloat in many parts of the world. His memory recalls many anecdotes of well-known men, and he was honoured with the personal friendship of the late King Edward VII. and of the German Emperor, by whom his seamanship, as well as his social qualities, were highly esteemed. As a sportsman he has something to say about shooting, fishing, hunting, and cricket, and his stories of life in the great country houses where he was a frequent guest have a flavour of their own.

LONDON: EDWARD ARNOLD, 41 & 43, MADDOX STREET, W.

NOVELS.

HOWARDS END.

By E. M. FORSTER,
Author of 'A Room with a View,' 'The Longest Journey,' etc.
6s.

BY THE SAME AUTHOR.

A ROOM WITH A VIEW. 6s.

THE RETURN.

By WALTER DE LA MARE.
6s.

'The Return' is the story of a man suddenly confronted, as if by the caprice of chance, with an ordeal that cuts him adrift from every certain hold he has upon the world immediately around him. He becomes acutely conscious of those unseen powers which to many, whether in reality or in imagination, are at all times vaguely present, haunting life with their influences. In this solitude—a solitude of the mind which the business of everyday life confuses and drives back—he faces as best he can, and gropes his way through his difficulties, and wins his way at last, if not to peace, at least to a clearer and quieter knowledge of self.

THE GRAY MAN.

By JANE WARDLE.
6s.

The writer is one of the very few present-day novelists who have consistently followed up the aim they originally set themselves—that of striking a mean between the Realist and the Romanticist. In her latest novel, 'The Gray Man,' which Miss Wardle herself believes to contain the best work she has so far produced, it will be found that she has as successfully avoided the bald one-sidedness of miscalled 'Realism' on the one hand, as the sloppy sentimentality of the ordinary 'Romance' on the other. At the same time, 'The Gray Man' contains both realism and romance in full measure, in the truer sense of both words.

BY THE SAME AUTHOR.

MARGERY PIGEON. 6s.

THE PASQUE FLOWER. 6s.

THE PURSUIT.

By FRANK SAVILE.
6s.

That the risk of being kidnapped, to which their great riches exposes multi-millionaires, is a very real one, is constantly being reaffirmed in the reports that are published of the elaborate precautions many of them take to preserve their personal liberty. In its present phase, where there is the great wealth on one side and a powerful gang—or rather syndicate—of clever rascals on the other, it possesses many characteristics appealing to those who enjoy a good thrilling romance. Mr. Savile has already won his spurs in this field, but his new tale should place him well in the front ranks of contemporary romancers.

BY THE SAME AUTHOR.

SEEKERS. *A Romance of the Balkans.* 6s.

THE DESERT VENTURE. 6s.
ANNE DOUGLAS SEDGWICK'S LATEST NOVEL.

FRANKLIN KANE.

By ANNE DOUGLAS SEDGWICK,
Author of 'Valerie Upton,' 'Amabel Channice,' etc.
Second Impression. 6s.

'Anne Sedgwick is in the first rank of modern novelists, and nobody who cares for good work can afford to miss one line that she writes.'—*Punch.*

'A figure never to be forgotten.'—*Standard.*

'There are no stereotyped patterns here.'—*Daily Chronicle.*

'A very graceful and charming comedy.'—*Manchester Guardian.*
AN ADMIRABLE NOVEL BY A NEW WRITER.

A STEPSON OF THE SOIL.

By MARY J. H. SKRINE.
Second Impression. 6s.

'Mrs. Skrine's admirable novel is one of those unfortunately rare books which, without extenuating the hard facts of life, maintain and raise one's belief in human nature. The story is simple, but the manner of its telling is admirably uncommon. Her portraits are quite extraordinarily vivid.'—*Spectator.*

LONDON: EDWARD ARNOLD, 41 & 43, MADDOX STREET, W.

BOOKS ON COUNTRY LIFE.

FLY-LEAVES FROM A FISHERMAN'S DIARY.

By CAPTAIN G. E. SHARP.
With Photogravure Illustrations. Crown 8vo., 5s. net.

This is a very charming little book containing the reflections on things piscatorial of a 'dry-fly' fisherman on a south country stream. Although the Author disclaims any right to pose as an expert, it is clear that he knows well his trout, and how to catch them. He is an enthusiast, who thinks nothing of cycling fifteen miles out for an evening's fishing, and home again when the 'rise' is over. Indeed, he confesses that there is no sport he loves so passionately, and this love of his art—surely dry-fly fishing is an art?—makes for writing that is pleasant to read, even as Isaac Walton's love thereof inspired the immortal pages of 'The Compleat Angler.'

MEMORIES OF THE MONTHS.

By the RIGHT HON. SIR HERBERT MAXWELL, Bart.,
Author of 'Scottish Gardens,' etc.
SERIES I. to V.
With Photogravure Illustrations. Large crown 8vo., 7s. 6d. each.

Every year brings new changes in the old order of Nature, and the observant eye can always find fresh features on the face of the Seasons. Sir Herbert Maxwell goes out to meet Nature on the moor and loch, in garden and forest, and writes of what he sees and feels. This is what gives his work its abiding charm, and makes these memories fill the place of old friends on the library bookshelf.

COLONEL MEYSEY-THOMPSON'S HANDBOOKS.

A HUNTING CATECHISM.

By COLONEL R. F. MEYSEY-THOMPSON,
Author of 'Reminiscences of the Course, the Camp, and the Chase.'
Fcap. 8vo., 3s. 6d. net.

A FISHING CATECHISM. 3s. 6d. net.

A SHOOTING CATECHISM. 3s. 6d. net.

A GAMEKEEPER'S NOTE-BOOK.

By Owen Jones and Marcus Woodward .
With Photogravure Illustrations.
Large crown 8vo., cloth, 7s. 6d. net.

In this charming and romantic book we follow the gamekeeper in his secret paths, stand by him while with deft fingers he arranges his traps and snares, watch with what infinite care he tends his young game through all the long days of spring and summer—and in autumn and winter garners with equal eagerness the fruits of his labour. He takes us into the coverts at night, and with him we keep the long vigil—while poachers come, or come not.

The authors know their subject through and through. This is a real series of studies from life, and the notebook from which all the impressions are drawn and all the pictures painted is the real note-book of a real gamekeeper.

TEN YEARS OF GAME-KEEPING.

By Owen Jones .
With numerous Illustrations from Photographs by the Author.
One volume, demy 8vo., cloth, 10s. 6d. net.

'This is a book for all sportsmen, for all who take an interest in sport, and for all who love the English woodlands. Mr. Jones writes from triple viewpoints—those of sportsman, naturalist, and gamekeeper—and every page of his book reveals an intimate knowledge of the ways of the English wild, a perfect mastery of all that the word "woodcraft" may stand for, and a true instinct of sportsmanship. This book at once takes its place as a standard work; and its freshness will endure as surely as spring comes to the woods that inspired it.'— *Evening Standard.*

REGINALD FARRER'S GARDENING BOOKS.

IN A YORKSHIRE GARDEN.

By REGINALD FARRER.
With numerous Illustrations. Demy 8vo. , 10s. 6d. net.

MY ROCK-GARDEN.

Fully Illustrated. Large crown 8vo., 7s. 6d. net. Third Impression.

ALPINES AND BOG-PLANTS.

Fully Illustrated. Large crown 8vo., 7s. 6d. net.

A BOOK ABOUT ROSES.

By the late Very Rev. S. Reynolds Hole , Dean of Rochester.
Illustrated by G. H. Moon and G. S. Elgood , R.I.
Twenty-fourth Impression. Presentation Edition, with Coloured Plates, 6s. Popular Edition, 3s. 6d.

A BOOK ABOUT THE GARDEN AND THE GARDENER.

By the late Very Rev. S. Reynolds Hole , Dean of Rochester.
Popular Edition. Crown 8vo., 3s. 6d.
    LONDON: EDWARD ARNOLD, 41 & 43, MADDOX STREET, W.

BOOKS OF TRAVEL.

FOREST LIFE AND SPORT IN INDIA.

By Sainthill Eardley-Wilmot , C.I.E., lately Inspector-General of Forests to the Indian Government; Commissioner under the Development and Road Improvement Funds Act.
Fully Illustrated. Demy 8vo. 12s. 6d. net.

The Author of this volume was appointed to the Indian Forest Service in days when the Indian Mutiny was fresh in the minds of his companions, and life in the department full of hardships, loneliness, and discomfort. These drawbacks, however, were largely compensated for by the splendid opportunities for sports of all kinds which almost every station in the Service offered, and it is in describing the pursuit of game that the most exciting episodes of the book are to be found. Tigers, spotted deer, wild buffaloes, mountain goats, sambhar, bears, and panthers, are the subject of endless yarns, in the relation of which innumerable useful hints, often the result of failure and even disasters, are given.

IN FORBIDDEN SEAS:
Recollections of Sea-Otter Hunting in the Kurils.

By H. J. Snow , F.R.G.S.
Illustrated. Demy 8vo. 12s. 6d. net.

The Author of this interesting book has had an experience probably unique in an almost unknown part of the world. The stormy wind-swept and fog-bound regions of the Kuril Islands, between Japan and Kamchatka, have rarely been visited save by the adventurous hunters of the sea-otter, and the animal is now becoming so scarce that the hazardous occupation of these bold voyagers is no longer profitable.

SPORT AND NATURE IN SPAIN.

By Abel Chapman and Walter J. Buck , British Vice-Consul at Jerez.
With 200 Illustrations by the Authors, E. Caldwell , and others, Sketch Maps, and Photographs.

In Europe Spain is certainly far and away the wildest of wild lands—due as much to her physical formation as to any historic or racial causes. Naturally the Spanish fauna remains one of the richest and most varied in Europe. It is of these wild regions and of their wild inhabitants that the authors write, backed by lifelong experience. The present work represents nearly forty years of constant study, of practical experience in field and forest, combined with systematic note-taking and analysis by men who are recognized as specialists in their selected pursuits. These comprise every branch of sport with rod, gun, and rifle; and, beyond all that, the ability to elaborate the results in the light of modern zoological science.

TWENTY YEARS IN THE HIMALAYA.

By Major the Hon. C. G. Bruce , M.V.O., Fifth Gurkha Rifles.
Fully Illustrated. With Map. Demy 8vo. , cloth. 16s. net.

The Himalaya is a world in itself, comprising many regions which differ widely from each other as regards their natural features, their fauna and flora, and the races and languages of their inhabitants. Major Bruce's relation to this world is absolutely unique—he has journeyed through it, now in one part, now in another, sometimes mountaineering, sometimes in pursuit of big game, sometimes in the performance of his professional duties, for more than twenty years; and now his acquaintance with it under all its diverse aspects, though naturally far from complete, is more varied and extensive than has ever been possessed by anyone else.

RECOLLECTIONS OF AN OLD MOUNTAINEER.

By Walter Larden .
Fully Illustrated. Demy 8vo., cloth. 14s. net.

There are a few men in every generation, such as A. F. Mummery and L. Norman Neruda, who possess a natural genius for mountaineering. The ordinary lover of the mountains reads the story of their climbs with admiration and perhaps a tinge of envy, but with no thought of following in their footsteps—such feats are not for him. The great and special interest of Mr. Larden's book lies in the fact that he does not belong to this small and distinguished class. He tells us, and convinces us, that he began his Alpine career with no exceptional endowment of nerve or activity, and describes, fully and with supreme candour, how he made himself into what he very modestly calls a second-class climber—not 'a Grepon-crack man,' but one capable of securely and successfully leading a party of amateurs over such peaks as Mont Collon or the Combin.

THE MISADVENTURES OF A HACK CRUISER.

By F. Claude Kempson ,
Author of 'The *Green Finch* Cruise.'
With 50 Illustrations from the Author's sketches.
Medium 8vo., cloth. 6s. net.

Mr. Kempson's amusing account of 'The *Green Finch* Cruise,' which was published last year, gave deep delight to the joyous fraternity of amateur sailormen, and the success that book enjoyed has encouraged him to describe a rather more ambitious cruise he undertook subsequently. Mr. Kempson is not an expert, but he shows how anyone accustomed to a sportsman's life can, with a little instruction and common sense, have a thoroughly enjoyable time sailing a small boat. The book is full of 'tips and wrinkles' of all kinds, interspersed with amusing anecdotes and reflections. The Author's sketches are exquisitely humorous, and never more so than when he is depicting his own substantial person.

LONDON: EDWARD ARNOLD, 41 & 43, MADDOX STREET, W.

THE COTTAGE HOMES OF ENGLAND.

Charmingly Illustrated in Colour by Mrs. ALLINGHAM.
With 64 Full-page Coloured Plates from Pictures by HELEN ALLINGHAM, never before reproduced. 8vo. (9-1/2 in. by 7 in.), 21s. net. Also a limited Edition de Luxe, 42s. net.

A HISTORY OF THE LONDON HOSPITAL.

By E. W. MORRIS,
Secretary of the London Hospital.
With Illustrations. 6s. net.

'Besant long ago wrote "All Sorts and Conditions of Men," and won and built thereby the People's Palace. Here is a better book. Its people are real, its romance is facts, its palace is a hospital of a thousand beds.'—*Daily Telegraph.*

THE BOOK OF WINTER SPORTS.

With an Introduction by the Rt. Hon. the EARL OF LYTTON, and contributions from experts in various branches of sport.
Edited by EDGAR SYERS.
Fully Illustrated. Demy 8vo., 15s. net.

THE DUDLEY BOOK OF COOKERY AND HOUSEHOLD RECIPES.

By GEORGIANA, COUNTESS OF DUDLEY.
Handsomely printed and bound. Third Impression. 7s. 6d. net.

COMMON-SENSE COOKERY:

Based on Modern English and Continental Principles worked out in Detail.
By Colonel A. Kenney-Herbert .
Over 500 pages. Illustrated. 6s. net.
BY THE SAME AUTHOR.

FIFTY BREAKFASTS. 2s. 6d.

FIFTY LUNCHEONS. 2s. 6d.

FIFTY DINNERS. 2s. 6d.

LONDON: EDWARD ARNOLD, 41 & 43, MADDOX STREET, W.

Transcriber's Notes

Pages 148 and 149 : The words noted below are transliterations of the original Greek characters.
    Then spoke a Greek, 'The Isles of Greece!
What can compare with those?
[Greek: Thalassa]! and [Greek: Eurêka]!
[Greek: Rhododaktylos êôs]!'
'But the country of my childhood
Is the best that man may know,
Oh [Greek: didêmi] also [Greek: phêmi],
[Greek: Zôê mou sas agapô]!'